WHAT'S**IN**STYLE
WINDOW
TREATMENTS

WHAT'S INSTYLE
WINDOW
TREATMENTS

Megan Connelly

CREATIVE HOMEOWNER®, Upper Saddle River, New Jersey

Publisher: Natalie Chapman
Editorial Director: Timothy O. Bakke
Production Manager: Kimberly H. Vivas

Senior Editor, Home Decorating: Kathie Robitz
Editor, Home Decorating: Therese Hoehlein Cerbie
Associate Editor: Linda Stonehill
Photo Editor: Stanley Sudol
Copy Editor: Ellie Sweeney
Editorial Assistants: Dan Houghtaling, Sharon Ranftle
Indexer: Schroeder Indexing Services

Senior Designer: Glee Barre
Book Designer: Stephanie Phelan
Associate Book Designers: Virginia Rubel, Nancy Stamatopoulos
Cover Design: Glee Barre, Robert Strauch
Front Cover Photography: Robert Harding Picture Library
Back Cover Photography: (left and upper right) Giammarino and Dworkin; (lower right) Jessie Walker

Manufactured in the United States of America

Current Printing (last digit)
10 9 8 7 6 5 4 3 2

What's in Style—Window Treatments
Library of Congress Control Number: 2001090770
ISBN: 1-58011-111-4

CREATIVE HOMEOWNER®
A Division of Federal Marketing Corp.
24 Park Way, Upper Saddle River, NJ 07458
Web site: **www.creativehomeowner.com**

dedication

For Ray Connelly, my father and rock.

contents

INTRODUCTION   **8**

1   **CURTAINS & DRAPERIES**   **10**
From full-length formal panels to charming
casual cafés, today's fashion-forward designs offer
an alluring range of possibilities.

2   **SHADES, BLINDS & SHUTTERS**   **24**
Searching for the ultimate in privacy and light
control without sacrificing style? Handsome
shades, blinds, and shutters are the answer.

3   **VALANCES & CORNICES**   **38**
The right top treatment can be one element
in a window's ensemble—or all of it, depending
on the overall design and your practical needs.

4   **SWAGS & JABOTS**   **50**
Running the gamut from tailored to blousy,
classic swags and jabots look chic on almost any
type of window.

5   **DECORATIVE HARDWARE**   **64**
Good-looking hardware can add a strong style
note to an interior design. Today's choices come
in many styles and finishes.

6   **FINISHING TOUCHES**   **76**
Baubles, bangles, and beads, plus traditional
trimmings, can accentuate a pretty curtain or
dress a simple shade.

7   **CHALLENGES & SOLUTIONS**   **90**
The shape, size, or location of some windows can
make them difficult to dress. Here are some
solutions to your window challenges.

8   **MINIMAL LOOKS**   **104**
If your taste is for contemporary or spare design,
you'll love the pared-down ideas for windows
presented in this chapter.

Resources   **114**   Index   **122**

Glossary   **118**   Credits   **127**

introduction

Windows are key **components** of a room, and selecting the most **appropriate** treatments for them will **enrich** the **design** of both the windows and the **room.**

Window treatments serve decorative and practical functions, both of which should hold equal sway when you're budgeting your decorating dollars. Ignoring one or the other will mean spending more money and time to remedy or replace a mistake. How does a professional decorator walk into a room and quickly determine the best way to dress a window, while the rest of us can spend months being unable to make a decision about a curtain, blind, or hardware? The answer is that a designer knows how to size up a window as well as the best available options.

While you don't always need a decorator's help to choose attractive and functional window treatments, you do need information and inspiration. *What's in Style—Window Treatments* offers plenty of both. It presents the latest window fashions with advice for using them to your home's best advantage. Turning these pages, you'll be motivated by an array of designs, clearly described and beautifully photographed in various settings. And whether you're buying custom- or ready-mades, or making your own, you'll find what you need to fit your style and budget.

The opening chapters demystify and showcase various styles of "soft" and "hard" window treatments. Chapter One covers all types of curtain and drapery styles, from café curtains to floor-length panels puddled on the floor, with plain, gathered, pleated, or tabbed headings, and ends with advice on which fabrics will work best. Because these treatments are made from fabric, they are often referred to as "soft" window dressings. Chapter Two explains the differences between shades, blinds, and shutters, often designated as "hard" window treatments. Although many times a shade, blind, or shutter sits below a soft treatment, each can stand alone. This chapter also explains how to take accurate measurements so that all of your window treatments will fit properly. Chapters Three and Four cover valances, cornices, swags, and jabots, otherwise known as top treatments. Sometimes a top treatment alone is enough window dressing. At other times a valance or swag is the crowning touch over panels or a shade or blind.

Need help in selecting the best drapery rod, pole and finials, or curtain holdbacks? Chapter Five gives the inside track on the latest decorative hardware that will fit and enhance your window treatment. Chapter Six presents the various ways that the additional flourishes and trims—rosettes, tassels, and tiebacks, to name a few—can give your window treatment a special finishing touch that sets it apart from all the rest.

Do you have a window—a bay, casement, or dormer, for example—that's a challenge to treat? Chapter Seven offers solutions that will not only dress the window with style but also enhance it. Or perhaps your room calls for a window treatment that minimizes fuss. In Chapter Eight you'll find ideas that emphasize the texture, lines, and space in the room, steering clear of unnecessary trims and embellishments.

What's in Style—Window Treatments covers both the decorative and practical aspects of window treatments right down to choosing the best hardware and the perfect tiebacks and trimmings. Whether your taste is formal or casual, traditional or contemporary, armed with the facts and this portfolio of styles and ideas, you'll find just what you're looking for to make your windows dramatic focal points and important supporting elements in your home's interior design.

1

curtains &
draperies

Curtain and drapery **treatments**
offer many **options** for decorating
all **styles** and types of windows.

Stylish and effective window treatments are no longer limited to off-the-rack, formal pinch-pleated draperies for the living room and to de rigueur frilly cotton tieback curtains for the kitchen and bathroom. A look at the latest curtain and drapery fashions will convince you that there is an enormous variety of brilliant choices for dressing windows in all the rooms of your home. Not only can you can choose from exciting adaptations on traditional window treatment styles, but for a completely personalized look you can also combine custom-ordered and ready-made components.

Although the terms "curtain" and "drapery" are often used interchangeably, drapery typically refers to heavier, formal lined panels, while curtains may be comparatively lightweight, unlined, and less formal. The style of the room and your needs for privacy, light control, and insulation will affect your choice. For a bright, airy look, sheer panels might suffice. But if you prefer a formal treatment, draperies drawn closed with a cord system can make the outside world all but disappear. Think about your objectives as you review the types of panels and fabrics available.

When choosing a curtain or drapery, also consider the style of its heading. The heading is the top part of a curtain or drapery, constructed in one of many ways to accommodate a pole or rod. In a sense, it turns a simple run of fabric into a curtain or drapery panel and gives it a particular style. For this reason, choosing the right type of heading for your panel is just as important as selecting the appropriate fabric or color.

PANELS

The basic unit of all curtains and draperies is the panel. Panels vary in length and heading style and come in virtually any kind of material, from velvet to voile. You can buy ready-made single panels, but most conventional treatments require two panels per window opening.

Lined panels fall under the drapery category. A lining enhances a panel's light-blocking and insulating ability and helps to define its shape. Although you'll often see white or beige linings, a patterned lining or one in a contrasting color can be pretty—especially when the curtain is pulled back. But remember that sunlight shining through a lightweight fabric can affect the color. An interlining is often used to separate two patterned layers and to prevent either design from showing through to the opposite side.

Panel Length

Although there are no set rules concerning the length of curtain or drapery panels, remember that the longer the treatment, the more formal it will look. But unless you're pulling together a traditional or period setting, you can determine the length to suit yourself, the style of the room, and the activity around the window. For instance, you don't want to block heat vents with heavy panels that fall to the floor.

The most common lengths for curtains and draperies are sill, below-sill, floor, and puddled.

Sill Length. These panels just graze the top of the windowsill. Windows that benefit from short, sill-length curtains or draperies include those arranged in a horizontal series, bay and bow windows, and windows that are frequently opened.

Tab-top striped drapery panels sport buttons to match the vibrant green lining. Sunlight passing through the floor-length panels projects the lining's color to the front of the draperies, adding depth to the overall look.

Below-Sill Length. Curtains and draperies should fall at least 4 inches below the window frame to conceal the apron. But if they fall too low, they may look awkward or unfinished. Below-sill-length treatments look great on picture windows and over window seats.

Floor Length. A treatment this long can dress a room with the elegance of an evening gown. Be sure it falls to exactly ½ inch from the floor, and when using layered panels, keep the back panels ¼ to ½ inch shorter than the front panels. If you'll need to open and close these long treatments, install the proper hardware, such as a traverse rod or a pole with rings.

Puddled. This highly dramatic effect is particularly appropriate for floor-to-ceiling treatments in formal rooms. It requires an extra 6 to 8 inches of fabric because you'll be turning the hem under and arranging the rest in gentle poufs on the floor. Unless you want to rearrange the curtains frequently, restrict this treatment to low-traffic areas; don't puddle panels that you plan to open and close frequently.

Café and Tiered Curtains

Café curtain panels cover just the lower part of a window. Whether alone or paired with a simple valance, café curtains look casual. And because they leave the upper portion of the window mostly bare, café curtains allow natural light to enter a room while offering partial privacy. Tiered curtains, or tiers, also are informal but provide more coverage.

HEADINGS

Because the heading of a curtain or drapery accommodates the pole or rod, its style reveals the type of hanging hardware it requires. Also, by considering the spacing between its gathers, pleats,

Café and tiered curtains, above and below left, are great for providing adjustable light and privacy control. **The sheer floor-length curtain panels,** opposite, reduce glare and offer some privacy when closed.

tabs, loops, or ties, you'll be able to tell how the panel will drape and fall.

Pocket Headings

The simplest and most common heading style is the rod-pocket heading. Here, a double row of stitching forms the casing for a curtain rod or pole. The top of the rod pocket may rest on the rod or, in the case of a ruffled heading, can extend 2 to 4 inches above it. Rod-pocket headings work well for curtains that don't often need to be pulled aside. If your panels will remain apart, exposing the rod, try bridging the gap between panels with a coordinating rod sleeve.

Gathered Headings

Behind a gathered heading, you may find a draw-cord strip that was used to shirr the fabric evenly. Rings or hooks connect this type of heading to the rod. Shallow, gathered headings look subtle, whereas deep gathers appear more dramatic. Full gathers can be bunched some more and sewn, taking the place of another top treatment.

Pleated Headings

Pleated headings give panels a tailored, formal appearance and add shaping to the fabric, which drapes in folds down its length. Pleats have many varieties. A pinch pleat, for example, is a large pleat subdivided into three smaller pleats. Divided in two, a simple pleat becomes a butterfly pleat. A fan pleat is a large, simple pleat extending above the top of the panel with two or four smaller pleats forming fanlike projections to either side. Narrow pencil pleats are spaced closely together. A goblet pleat consists of a 2- to 4-inch-wide tube pinched together at its base, and a button may highlight the pinch-point. A line of stitching flattens and secures the bases of cartridge pleats.

Floor-length draperies grace this master bedroom. To control light and privacy, install panels like these on a traverse rod or a pole with rings that allow you to open and close curtains easily.

Flat Headings

Tabbed, tied, plain, and pierced headings are considered flat headings. With these headings, the rod or pole is as important as the fabric because the rod is always visible. **Tab and Tie Tops.** These consist of loops spaced about 4 inches apart across the panel. Made of fabric, ribbon, or cord to match or contrast with the panel, both ends of each loop are usually sewn into the heading. One style has a free end with a buttonhole that slips over a button sewn to the heading. Tied loops are formed with ribbons or fabric strips sewn into the heading.

Pulled-back panels, above and left, frame these seating areas. The fabrics help set the tone. **A simple rod-pocket panel,** opposite, hung and tied back with twine, is the perfect dressing for this cabin window.

Plain or Pierced Headings. These panels hang from rings or holes made in the heading. Curtain rings or café clips, threaded on a rod, often secure panels having plain headings. A pierced heading is a series of evenly spaced, reinforced holes—buttonholes or grommets—that range along the top of the panel. Like pleated headings, pierced headings benefit from the use of buckram or interfacing. The pierced heading threads easily onto a rod as long as the holes in the panel are larger than the rod's diameter. You also can thread ties through a pierced heading to attach it to the rod.

Unusual but beautiful fabrics, left and below left, can become stunning curtains. Beaded fringe on the lower one adds special detail. **The shaped heading** of the panel below uses snaps to fasten it around a metal pole.

Design Tip

Follow length guidelines for foolproof results, but remember that they're not rules. Go ahead and play with curtain and drapery lengths. Instead of shortening long panels at the hem, for instance, take up excess material by blousing them over tiebacks for a pleasing effect.

Fabric Types

The pattern and texture of your window treatment will be in the limelight, and more than headings, panel type, or length, it's the fabric that everyone will notice first. Surprisingly, fabric is also the element that affords you the most leeway. While it's easy to pick a print that suits your design, the fabric itself may not be the correct choice. The information in the table below will familiarize you with the traditional uses of a variety of materials. The care instructions included in the table are good guidelines, but follow the cleaning instructions given by the manufacturer for any fabric you choose. In addition, always test a sample before cleaning the entire curtain or drapery.

Fabric	Use	Care
Brocade: Weighty fabric in silk, wool, cotton, or a combination featuring a raised (jacquard) design	Draperies and top treatments	Cotton: Machine wash cold / tumble dry low / expect shrinkage Silk: Dry clean only Wool: Dry clean only
Cambric: Plain, tightly woven cotton or linen having a sheen on one side	Curtains	Linen: Dry cleaning preferred Hand wash / line dry / may shrink Cotton: Machine wash cold / tumble dry low / expect shrinkage / may lose sheen
Canvas: Coarse, woven cotton. Can be heavy- or lightweight	Curtains, draperies, and shades	Machine wash cold / tumble dry low / expect shrinkage
Chintz: Cotton, all-over print fabric, often floral. Coated with a resin that gives it a sheen	Curtains, draperies, and top treatments	Dry clean only to maintain sheen
Damask: A material made with cotton, silk, wool, or a combination of these fibers with a satin raised (jacquard) design	Draperies and top treatments	See Brocade
Gingham: Plain-woven cotton fabric with block or checked prints	Curtains, draperies, and trimmings	Machine wash cold / tumble dry low / expect shrinkage
Lace: Cotton or a cotton and polyester material featuring open-worked designs	Curtains, top treatments, and shades	Some dry clean only Machine wash cold / gentle cycle / line dry / may shrink
Linen: Strong fabric made from flax. Creases easily	Curtains, draperies, and shades	Dry cleaning preferred Hand wash / line dry / expect shrinkage
Moiré: Acetate or silk fabric having a wavy, watermark pattern	Draperies	Dry clean only
Muslin: A coarse, plain-woven cotton in white or cream. Often sheer	Curtains	Machine wash cold / tumble dry low / expect shrinkage
Organdy: Light cotton washed in acid for a crisp finish	Curtains, top treatments, and trimmings	Dry clean only
Satin: A cotton, linen, or silk fabric with a glossy surface and dull back, sometimes with a moiré finish	Draperies and top treatments	Dry clean only
Silk: A soft, shiny fabric made from the fine fibers produced by silkworms	Draperies and top treatments	Dry cleaning preferred Hand wash / line dry / expect shrinkage
Taffeta: Acetate or silk fabric that appears shiny and maintains shape	Draperies, top treatments, and trimmings	Dry clean only
Toile de Jouy: Cotton or linen printed with pastoral scenes	Curtains, draperies, and top treatments	Dry clean only
Velvet: Cotton, silk, polyester, or viscose rayon fabric with a smooth, iridescent-looking pile	Draperies	Dry clean only

Choose panel style, length, and fabric to complement the room and window.

"Clothes make the man," or woman, and curtains and draperies can make the window—even the room. Window fashions, in fact, are a lot like couture. Today's renditions tend to be simpler, lighter, and less fussy than ones in recent years.

shades, blinds & shutters

Today's **attractive** shades, blinds, and shutters look fabulous **alone** or **paired** with other treatments.

Whether installed by themselves, combined with curtain or drapery panels, or paired with a treatment spanning the top of the window, shades, blinds, and shutters give you the power to easily control the amount of light and privacy you want in that particular room. While a particular type of shade—the plain white vinyl roller shade—is still practical and very serviceable in certain situations, it does not offer the style and versatility of all the different types of shades, blinds, and shutters on the market today. Because they come in a range of styles, share materials, and frequently are misnamed by their manufacturers, it's often hard to distinguish between shades and blinds and sometimes even between blinds and shutters.

A shade, constructed from a single piece of fabric or vinyl, regulates light and privacy by the amount it is raised or lowered via a cord system or a spring-tension roller. Blinds, either the horizontal or vertical type, adjust light and privacy levels as they are lowered or closed and as the angle of their movable slats is adjusted. While these slats once were made strictly of wood, metal, or plastic, today they may be vinyl or covered in fabric. Shutters installed with hinges swing and fold open and closed. Some have adjustable louvers that regulate the light in almost the same way blinds do. Others are merely hinged frames that can be fitted with the material of your choice. All of these types of window treatments are available as ready-mades or can be custom-made to fit your particular window or door.

SHADES

Shades fall into six groups—roller shades, Roman shades, festoon shades, pleated shades, cellular shades, and woven-wood, or natural, shades. A shade's ability to block light depends on its material, and pale or lightweight shades may be lined. Whichever shade you choose, make sure that it not only looks good but suits your needs for privacy and light control.

Roller Shades

Roller shades are spring-operated. They come in vinyl, textured or plain fabric, and an array of colors, making these simplest of shades an attractive option. A fancy hem design—scalloped, fringed, ruffled, or notched and fitted with a rod—can change a shade's personality to anything from elegant to whimsical.

Roman Shades

Streamlined Roman shades feature flat, horizontal pleats that may be 4 to 6 inches deep. You operate them with a cord and, like roller shades, they are available in a variety of colors and materials. A Roman shade can be made from a single layer of fabric, or it may be lined.

Festoon Shades

Festoon shades are especially decorative, and their opulent gathers appear soft and feminine. Styles include balloon shades, cloud shades, and Austrian shades. Some festoon shades are operable or adjustable, but many are stationary.

Pleated Shades

Made of permanently folded paper or fabric, pleated shades stack compactly enough to be nearly invisible under curtains. Some of these shades have a double cord system that lets you lower the shades from the top and

Fabrics and cord systems define the style of Roman shades, above and below left. **Roman shades,** right, offer light and privacy control for this breakfast bay.

raise them from the bottom. You can rest them up, down, or somewhere in between. Because pleated shades have 1- to 2-inch-wide pleats, they usually look best in solid colors: some incorporate texture or a tone-on-tone pattern for variety. Retailers also offer pleated shades with room-darkening or insulating properties.

Cellular Shades

Cellular, or honeycomb, shades feature layers of fabric that are pleated accordion-style and joined, back to back, at the pleat valleys. Newer versions of honeycomb shades have no exposed cords and operate like roller shades. Although cellular shades resemble pleated shades, their air-cushioned fabric layers provide better UV protection and superlative insulation.

Woven-Wood Shades

Sometimes called natural shades and often referred to as blinds, this category of window coverings includes shades made from bamboo, matchsticks, hemp, jute, woven reeds, grasses, and other natural or natural-looking materials. Natural shades are operated with rollers or cords, and the tightness of their weave determines their light-blocking capability.

BLINDS

Blinds, which come in a range of materials, have either horizontal or vertical slats. Their linear quality complements contemporary settings, but they also enhance traditional rooms when they are paired with curtains or draperies.

Venetian Blinds

Venetian blinds feature convex horizontal slats that vary in width from $\frac{1}{2}$ to 3 inches. You can raise and lower the

Woven-wood shades fit right in with this room setting. The lines and geometric shapes displayed by the light passing through the shades add even more interest.

slats with a cord or keep the blind in the lowered position and adjust the angle of the slats to direct light.

Commonly made of aluminum, vinyl, or wood, standard-width Venetian blinds come in a variety of colors, while custom blinds may have pearlized, metallic, suedelike, or other specialty finishes. Custom-made blinds also offer decorative ladder tapes in $1/2$- to 1-inch widths that cover the cords joining the slats.

Venetian blinds made of wood feature natural, stained, or painted slats. Because they are thicker than metal and plastic blinds, wood blinds don't stack as compactly. You can purchase wood blinds with squared or rounded slats, decorative ladder tapes, and even coordinating cornices that conceal the top of the blind. Faux-wood blinds constructed from PVC offer the look of wood blinds for less expense. Sometimes blinds must be custom-ordered, but they also come in standard sizes.

Special pleated shades, left, can be lowered from the top and raised from the bottom. Most, as those above, only move up. **A shutter,** right, is adjusted with tilt bar.

Measuring Windows

Correct measurements will help you determine whether ready-made options will work for you. Without them, you cannot accurately price the elements you need. Use a metal measuring tape for accuracy and record the measurements on paper. See "Inside or Outside Mount," page 34, for more advice.

Inside Mount for Shades, Blinds, and Tension Rods

Inside the window frame, measure the width across the top, center, and bottom. Use the narrowest measurement, and round down to the nearest ⅛ inch. Measure the height of the window from the top of the opening to the sill.

Outside Mount for Shades, Blinds, Cornices, or Curtain or Drapery Rods or Poles

Figure out the amount of space on each side of the window and above and below the window that you want to cover with your treatment. Then decide on bracket placement—on the window frame or the wall.

- Professionals recommend that outside-mounted shades or blinds extend 2 inches beyond the window sash on each side.
- To determine the appropriate rod length, measure from bracket to bracket. For a decorative pole with finials, add 5 to 8 inches on each side; the actual amount depends on the finial style. Be sure that you have enough room on either side of window before you buy the pole and finials.
- For a fuller curtain look, the width of the panels you use should be at least twice the measurement from bracket to bracket. Some opulent looks call for fabric measuring three times the bracket-to-bracket measurement.
- To determine the appropriate length of curtain and drapery panels, measure from the bracket placement down to the top of the sill, to below the sill, or to the floor, depending on the length you desire. If the panel heading extends above the rod or pole, add that measurement to the length as well.

Vertical Blinds

While you can fit any window with vertical rather than horizontal blinds, vertical blinds suit very large windows and sliding doors particularly well. Vertical blinds' free-hanging slats, or vanes, are cord-controlled and move back and forth on a track, stacking neatly to one side. Slats come in many colors, and you can angle or close them to control light. Special textured slats mimic stucco designs, leather, linen, tweed, and crushed fabric. You may purchase optional coordinating valances, really just heading strips, to conceal hardware.

Natural shades with valances dress the windows and door, above. Those at the windows are set inside the window frame, leaving the decorative trimwork exposed.

Fabric slats, which contain a stiffener, can hang free or slide into channeled vinyl casings that increase their durability, light-blocking ability, and price. These casings cover only the back of each slat, hooking over the edges to be barely visible from the front. Transparent casings display the slat back, while solid-color casings present a uniform appearance to passersby.

SHUTTERS

The weight and permanence of shutters almost qualify them as architectural embellishments. While shutters function like shades or blinds, they control light more effectively. Shutters feature flat or louvered panels or fabric panels set into a frame, and they look

Design Tip

While decorative hems add interest to roller shades, they also increase the cost. If you're handy with a glue gun, choose one of the trims available at fabric and craft stores, and consider attaching it yourself. Give your shades fancy pulls for an inexpensive dash of pizzazz.

Wooden shutters are a bold statement for any window. These stained shutters, near right, are installed on top of the window frame; those painted white, opposite, are set inside the frame.

Inside or Outside Mount

Sometimes you have an option of installing a shade or blind on the inside or outside surface of the window frame. Often the decision is based on whether you are buying stock items, which are available in a limited number of sizes, or custom-made treatments. When deciding where to install your blind or shade, take accurate measurements of the window and blind or shade, and use the information below as guidelines.

Outside Mount

- May be necessary if buying a stock item that will not fit the inside width measurement across the window frame
- May be necessary if the window frame is not deep enough to contain at least the shade or blind mounting brackets, if not the entire depth of the unit
- Can compensate for unattractive or nonexistent window trim
- Can make a too narrow window look wider

Inside Mount

- Cannot be used if the blind or shade will not fit within the inside measurements of the window opening
- Is recommended if the blind or shade will be covered by draw curtains or draperies, which may be impeded by the shade or blind
- Allows handsome trimwork around the window to remain visible
- Can make a wide window appear narrower

handsome alone or when paired with a soft treatment. Because they become part of the window, shutters look best when painted or finished the same as the rest of the window frame. You can mount shutters inside or outside the window frame, but wide windows may require extra framing to support the shutters.

Louvered Shutters

These shutters may feature a tilt bar that is used to angle the louvers to control and direct light. Vertical louvered shutters have 1- to 1¼-inch-wide louvers that may pivot from side to side. Plantation shutters fill the window opening and feature 2- to 4-inch-wide horizontal louvers that may tilt up and down. Café shutters cover just half of the window—usually the lower portion. Double-hung tiered sets can cover a window, giving you more ways to regulate the light and privacy.

Panel Shutters

In place of louvers, panel shutters feature solid, inoperable panels that you need to open to admit light or air. Panel shutters commonly consist of flat wood or a fabric or paper insert that blocks or filters sunlight.

Shades, blinds, or shutters can suit all types and styles of rooms.

Concerned about the cost of custom shades, blinds, or shutters? Relax. You can find great-looking ones in many standard sizes, including ones to fit today's popular "architectural" windows. More versatile options include patterned and textured finishes and a range of colors. Installation in most cases is an easy do-it-yourself project.

3

valances & cornices

The **perfect** valance or cornice can transform an **ordinary** window into an **extraordinary** one.

A pelmet, the catchall term for valances and cornices, is a versatile decorating element that can establish the style or ambiance of your room. Though it's not essential, except in period rooms, a pelmet can be an attractive and useful feature in a room. For example, if your room scheme is contemporary, casual, or minimal, a simple chic top treatment—such as a gracefully gathered valance—will soften the lines of shutters or blinds. In richly decorated or traditional rooms, a cornice of crown molding can lend architectural importance to undistinguished windows, and opulent pelmets will balance elegant furnishings. Pelmets can also be used to cover worn window frames, conceal nondecorative hardware, and cap too tall windows, making them appear in better proportion to the room.

To ensure that your pelmet blends with the rest of the window treatment's design and doesn't overwhelm or dominate it, keep its proportion in mind. A pelmet should not be so short as to appear skimpy, and you'll naturally need longer ones for taller windows. Ideally, a valance won't be longer than one-quarter of the window's length, and the tails of a shaped valance should extend to one-third its length.

While searching for inspiration, look to the details within the room. For example, the colors in a stained-glass window could be in the fabric for a balloon valance. Or perhaps the simplicity of the elements in the room could be a perfect contrast for a box cornice decorated with tapestry and exquisite trim molding.

VALANCES

A valance is a soft top treatment made of fabric. It may dress a window by itself, coordinate with existing panels or café curtains, top a drapery treatment, or soften a hard top treatment, such as a cornice. Valances share some features with curtain and drapery panels. For example, valances attach to window hardware, as do curtains and draperies, and often have the same headings as curtains. An overview of valance types follows.

Balloon Valances

Like the balloon shade, a balloon valance features soft, romantic-looking poufs created by gathered material. But unlike the shade, this valance is stationary. One type of balloon valance, a puff valance, is basically one long pocket. You can pull apart its two layers to form a pouf, or stuff the opening with batting or tissue paper for more fullness. A cloud valance has more fullness at its scalloped bottom edge, and the Austrian valance features shirring evenly along most of its length.

Pleated Valances

The popular, traditional pleated valance is available in many varieties. Aside from its pleated heading, this tailored valance often has additional folds or gathers along its length. The box-pleat valance features uniform, hard-edged, inverted pleats. A pleated-and-gathered valance has a heading that features alternating pinch pleats and gathers; it falls more softly than a valance having box pleats, and appears more formal. Triple- and butterfly-pleat valances have pleated headings that release into soft folds. Bell-pleat valances consist of wide, soft cone-shaped pleats.

A plaid pelmet, upper left, combines an upholstered cornice and a gathered shaped valance. The simple valances, left, are tied to decorative rods. A series of rectangular panels outlined with contrasting trim form the unique valance and side panels, opposite.

Distinctive Valances

Valances that are both unique and beautifully decorative can be made from unconventional materials. If it's a material that you prefer not to cut, perhaps it can be draped and fastened around a pole or rod, or folded and stapled to a mounting board and then installed. When the material can be finished with a rod-pocket heading, it can be threaded onto a rod or pole and then installed across the window. Here are several suggestions.

- Hang graduated lengths of heavy, wide grosgrain ribbons side by side with their lower ends producing a shaped lower edge for the valance.
- Fold and drape a fringed shawl, points down, over a rod.
- Tie strings of beads or shells onto a rod and set it across the window.
- Use entire or partial pieces of lace or antique linens that have embroidery, monograms, decorative cutwork, or handmade trimmings. Some popular

choices might include all or part of a lace tablecloth, depending on the amount needed for the window. You might also consider pillowcases, kitchen towels, or hand towels for narrow windows or the upper portion of an embroidered or eyelet-trimmed flat bedsheet for wider windows. Several linen or cotton napkins or doilies, overlapping each other and with their corners pointing down, also make charming valances.

Tabbed Valances

A tabbed valance attaches to window hardware with loops, ties, or rings and, because it does not fully conceal the rod, needs attractive hardware. Gathered tabbed valances have a fuller appearance but must be at least one-and-a-half times the window's width. A tabbed valance with a shaped hem looks best when it's pulled flat. It should equal the width of the window.

Gathered Valances

A gathered valance is simply a rod-pocket valance that measures two to three times the width of the window. It may feature a ruffled heading or a shaped hem. Shirring the valance onto a rod creates its fullness. An arched rod can add a distinctive look to the top of a ruffled valance.

Toga Valances

A toga valance resembles a short curtain panel with rod pockets at both ends. The toga effect comes from alternating at least three panels—one of which may contrast with the others—on the rod. If, for example, you have two blue panels and one white panel, thread them onto the rod in this order: one end of the first blue panel, one end of the white panel, the free end of the first blue panel, one end of the second blue panel, the free end of the white panel, and the free end of the second blue panel. When installed, the white will overlap the blue.

CORNICES

A cornice is a hard, permanent valance that is usually made of wood embellished with architectural molding. Although it is designed to remain in place when curtains and draperies change, there is a trend toward creating cornices of softer materials to match specific curtains or draperies. If your cornice will add architectural detail, match it to nearby trim or keep it a neutral hue that will work with any window treatment.

Box Cornices

The box cornice consists of a face board (the front), two end boards (the sides), and a dust board (the top). The

---

Tasseled pennants, above, arranged in a mirror image, continue the eclectic theme of this room. The structured box cornice, opposite, is a handsome architectural feature.

Design Tip

If a box cornice appeals to you, consider embellishing it with classic architectural molding. For a look that will last through the years, use timeless molding styles—crown, egg-and-dart, dentil, rope, or scrolled leaf designs. Manufacturers often call these classic motifs by other names, but you'll quickly learn to recognize them.

basic box may be embellished with molding, then painted and mounted or draped with fabric swags. Sometimes a box cornice is upholstered and trimmed with tufting, pleats, buttons, or studs. A cornice may cap a fabric valance that softens its lower edge and gives it a finished, layered appearance.

Shaped Cornices

Typically, a shaped cornice consists of intricately cut panels of buckram-stiffened fabric attached to a cornice shelf. Painted or fabric-covered cardboard can also be used. A shaped cornice might feature scallops, notched designs, S-curves, or pendent shapes along its lower edge and be further embellished with moldings, piping, tassels, or bands of trim.

Lambrequins

A lambrequin cornice fits around the window and extends to the floor or at least two-thirds of the way down the sides of the window. Like a box cornice, a lambrequin usually consists of wooden sides, front panels, and a top that may be painted, stained, or upholstered.

A cornice with interesting fretwork, opposite, sits like a crown above majestic windows. **An attractive lace panel,** above left, is only a part of this window dressing that includes gingham wallpaper and hand-painted flowers. **A shaped cornice,** above, is edge-finished with piping.

Make a Simple Cornice

You can buy inexpensive kits for making cornices that also include instructions. Or you can make a quick-and-easy cornice using the instructions below. You will need

- Measuring tape
- Straightedge
- Foam core board
- Razor knife or box cutter
- Polyester batting
- Hot glue gun and glue sticks
- Scissors
- Fabric
- Staple gun
- Optional decorative trim

Decide the height of the cornice from its top to bottom edges. Measure across the top of the window and add double the depth of the return (the sides of the cornice). For example, if each side of the cornice will be 6 inches deep, add 12 inches to your window length measurement. Cut the foam core board to this total length by the desired height. Measure in from each end of the board the depth of each return, and using a straightedge, score the front of the board with the blade, being careful not to cut all the way through it. Bend the board back

along the score marks to create the returns. Cut batting to fit the front and both returns of the cornice, and glue it in place. Cut the fabric 2 or more inches larger than the cornice on all sides. Lay the fabric flat with its wrong side facing up, and place the batting side of the cornice onto the fabric. Pull the fabric evenly around the cornice, and glue or staple its edges to the back of the board. Wrap the cornice around the window frame, and staple it in place through the valance and into the window frame. Decorate the cornice with trim or other embellishments.

Design Tip

Any new cornice or cornice shelf includes mounting hardware and directions for its installation. But you'll probably need to purchase mounting brackets to install older or homemade cornices. If you're not comfortable with the idea of working on a ladder, especially while handling the cornice and various tools, call a pro. A professional installer will charge a flat rate for coming to your house plus an additional fee for each treatment. Prices vary, but your location, the size of the treatment (measured by the foot), and the difficulty of the job will determine its price.

The beautifully shaped cornice and the puddled drapery panel, opposite, mimic the curves of the Victorian settee, and the sequined medallions add more glamour to the overall setting. A box cornice embellished with a hand-painted mural, above, complements the crewel embroidery on the drapery panels.

A variety of styling techniques can be used for valances and cornices.

Valances and cornices have made a comeback in recent years. One reason is that they offer a clever way to disguise or enhance the size and shape of a window or tie together mismatched windows. For example, add height to a short opening with a cornice or valance that is installed on the wall above the window.

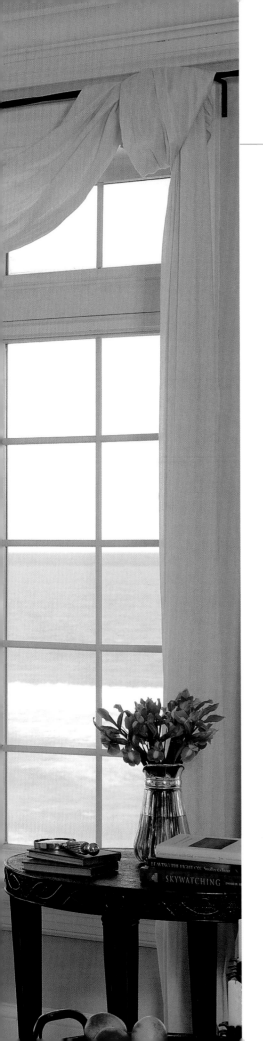

4

swags & jabots

Versatile swag-and-jabot combinations **provide** over-the-top **styling** in all types of rooms.

Depending on the fabric and style, swags and jabots can take on almost any personality from sophisticated to casual or something else in between. A triple-swag treatment of lined silk flanked by piped jabots, for instance, looks regal and very different from an unlined plain linen scarf swag draped over a decorative wood or metal rod.

If you've wondered about the difference between a swag and a valance, you're not alone—even professionals who make swags and valances use the terms interchangeably. While a valance can be any of a range of soft treatments for dressing the top of a window, a swag has a very distinct form. It may help to remember that swags are shaped like crescents, and one or more swags can span the top of the window.

Jabots are the side pieces, long or short, that flank the swag. They are often referred to as cascades, or tails. Historically, a swag-and-jabot top treatment accompanied drapery panels, curtain panels, and blinds. But today's more casual approach to window coverings invites you to use the treatment by itself or pair it with only a blind. Swag-and-jabot treatments also look beautiful framing French and sliding doors.

Whether you use them in modern or traditional ways, the arrangement of swags flanked by cascading jabots maintains its place as a favorite of good design. Although shaped valances and curtain panels that have angled sides may simulate jabots, they lack a crescent-shaped element and are therefore not considered to be a true swag-and-jabot treatment.

5

SWAGS & JABOTS

Traditional swag-and-jabot treatments that use heavy, lined drapery fabrics are affixed to a board mounted over the window. But stylish hardware, such as decorative rods and specially designed swag holders, lets you mount swags and jabots in different ways for a variety of styles. Some arrangements using single, double, triple, and fan swags are merely updates of traditional styles. Others, such as swagged or wrapped window scarves, are today's cutting-edge window fashions.

Swag Styles

Conventional swag-and-jabot treatments are made up of separate pieces and feature at least one swag with a jabot at each end. A modern version may be a single piece of material—a window scarf—draped over a rod or threaded through swag holders to form both the swag and jabots.

Beautiful ribbon-print fabric set over a white lining, above, draws attention to the view outside. **A classic layering** of fringed swags and jabots over drapery panels, above right, stands out in this traditional room setting. **Self-lined swag and jabots** outlined with trim soften a Venetian blind in the library, opposite.

Design Tip

The number of swags to drape across a window will depend on the width of the window and the look you want to achieve. When planning how many swags you'll need for the treatment, consider the following:

- The most popular arrangement is an uneven number of swags with the middle one spanning the center of the window.
- The width of a swag should not exceed 40 inches; its depth (drop) can range from 12 to 20 inches.
- Swags should overlap each other slightly.

Traditional swag-and-jabot treatments rely on balance and symmetry, which means that you'll see the same arrangement on each side of the window. These swags and jabots are usually pleated, share the same fabric, and are generally lined. Swags and jabots, however, though traditional in shape, often are made with coordinating or contrasting fabrics that, when of similar weight and texture, can still look balanced.

Single Swag. A single swag is simply one swag flanked by individual jabots. A fan swag features a single swag pleated at its top center so that soft folds radiate from it.

Double Swags. The double swag version features two adjacent swags. For an elegant variation on the double swag, you might try a crown swag: a fluted or pipe jabot at the center raised higher than the rest of the treatment separates the swags, which slope down to meet jabots at each end of the window. (See "Jabot Styles," page 59, for more information.)

Cornice-topped swags and jabots, left, fit right in with this window seat. **Stripes and plaids,** above and above right, are popular choices and can suit almost any style room.

Design Tip

While planning your swag-and-jabot treatment, draw the window to scale. Then, using tissue paper as an overlay, sketch possible treatments over the base drawing of the window. Vary the number, size, and depth of the swags; add jabots between the swags as well as at the ends of the treatment; and experiment with different lengths for the jabots.

Intricate folding and draping, above, complete with cord, produces a distinctive top treatment. Tasseled trim finishes the swags and jabots, right.

Design Tip

Plaids and stripes are a traditional choice for swags and jabots. But how they are folded and draped has a significant effect on the resulting overall pattern. For example, the lines can be positioned to be vertical and horizontal, or they can be draped as a diagonal. In addition, installing the darker-value stripes as the outer part of the pleat will create a totally different look from the one produced by setting the lighter value there. Try folding the fabric in different ways and pleat depths before you finally decide on the look that you prefer.

Three or More Swags. The center element of a triple swag might hang over the other two swags or is simply hung between them. Sometimes, the center swag is larger than the others are and drapes lower than those beside it. Regardless of the number of swags, each side will mirror the other in this symmetrical arrangement.

Jabot Styles

Traditional jabots, like conventional draperies, look formal and well tailored. The cascade jabot, which is cut on a diagonal and pleated at the top, is the most common style. A fluted jabot is an open tube with a straight lower edge. A pipe jabot is a tube with a pointed edge.

It's best to line most jabots, because pleats and folds may reveal their undersides. The tops of separate jabots may be displayed or hidden by a swag.

WINDOW SCARVES

A window scarf is one of the newer "tools" for creating beautiful and dramatic treatments for the top of a window. The scarf is basically a long length of fabric, but the manner in which it is hung and draped defines its resulting swag or wrapped-pole shape.

To create these relaxed, casual, and often romantic treatments, you'll need three key ingredients: a relatively generous length of fabric; the correct hardware; and a willingness to pull, primp, and reposition the fabric until you achieve the right look. A helper can make this job much easier. Make sure that your scarf is long enough to form generous jabots because without enough fabric, the arrangement will appear skimpy. For best results, use a lightweight fabric that has no right or wrong side. Fabrics such as voile, lace, and lawn work particularly well. They are also easy to work with and form graceful folds, drapes, and wraps.

A magnificent treatment, opposite, frames a row of simple windows. **A plaid scarf with a plain lining,** right, is casually draped over decorative brackets.

Hanging a Scarf Swag

- Arrange the fabric by laying it out on a large, clean surface and softly pleating it lengthwise, accordion-style.
- Estimate at which two points the fabric will begin to descend the sides of the window, and pin or tie the pleats in place at those points.
- Place your fabric over the pole, or thread it carefully through the brackets, positioning the jabots in place.
- Pull at the lower pleats in the center of the swag to create an even drape.
- Release the pins or ties from the tops of the jabots.
- Stand back and study the arrangement; then go back and make any adjustments.

Wrapping a Window Scarf

The best way to wrap a window scarf around a pole is as follows:

- Lay out the material on a large, clean surface. Gather the fabric at the top of each jabot, and use elastic to hold it together.
- Swing one jabot into place over the pole and, starting from there, wind the swag portion as many times as you need around the pole until you reach the elastic at the second jabot, which should have landed at the opposite end of the pole.
- Readjust wraps along the pole. Generally, wrapped swags just touch or slightly overlap each other.
- For a dramatic effect, stuff the wrapped swags with tissue paper or thin foam, depending on the translucence and weight of your fabric.
- Release elastics at tops of jabots.

Scarf Swags

A scarf swag is formed by draping a window scarf over brackets or a pole to create a look of a swag and jabots. Scarf swags look best when their jabots fall about two-thirds of the way to the sill. The draping need not be symmetrically arranged. An asymmetrical treatment—one jabot longer than the other—can be dramatic.

Because the scarf fabric will not cover the hardware completely, it's important to choose a pretty pole with finials, or decorative swag brackets for securing the scarf crescent at each end. Some brackets feature ornate

A sheer, self-lined scarf, left, is draped over brass swag holders. Notice the separate pipe jabot. **Fringed scarves,** above, are held at the center by a holdback and at

plasterwork; others are simply rings through which you can pull the scarf. There are also special brackets that come with instructions for forming rosettes or other decorative fabric folds around them.

Wrapped Scarves

A wrapped scarf produces swags and jabots when wrapped loosely around a pole; it can require even more fabric than a scarf swag. The weight of this extra fabric and the difficulty of wrapping it while standing on a ladder make this treatment more ambitious.

other points are threaded through decorative brackets. **Each fringed scarf,** right, is draped asymmetrically but when viewed as a pair form a symmetrical arrangement.

Swags and jabots of any styling can take center stage in a room.

A swag-and-jabot treatment suits almost any style interior or window. If a room is formal, a heavy, lined fabric in a traditional print is appropriate. Choose simple cottons, checks, plaids, or small prints for a country room. Sheers and asymmetrical swags pair best with contemporary or eclectic interiors.

5

decorative hardware

A marriage of function and form has produced a wide variety of decorative hardware.

Pretty poles with fancy finials, inventive swag or scarf holders, and ingenious holdbacks are just a few of today's window accessories. Now, instead of relying only on the color and pattern of your curtain fabric to set the tone for your window and room, you can let the hardware take a supporting or even a leading role. You won't have far to search for what you need, either. Decorative hardware is the heart and soul of today's window fashions, and the most up-to-date, sought-after looks are within easy reach of everyone. Divine inspiration or a resident carpenter need not be on hand to create all the intriguing window treatments you see in books and magazines. Many of them can be replicated after a visit to your favorite home, curtain, or fabric store.

While decorative hardware takes center stage in many of the contemporary window fashions, traditional treatments also benefit from today's innovative hardware. Drapery poles and their decorative ends, finials, draw the most attention, and for the most part, these poles work just like their functional forerunners. But made-to-be-seen rings, clips, and pins pick up where old-fashioned drapery hooks leave off.

Today's array of swag holders has revolutionized swag-and-jabot treatments, setting off entirely new categories of top treatments such as scarf swags and wrapped window scarves. Holdbacks, which often coordinate with a pole's finials, replace or are used in conjunction with tieback treatments. They can also be installed at the top of a window or door and serve as holders for scarf swags.

DECORATIVE POLES

You've made up your mind to use a decorative pole with finials. You scour the stores, cut out possible candidates from magazines and catalogs, and surf the Web for a pole that's just right for your room. When it comes time to narrowing down your favorites, however, you find

yourself looking at 50 pole and finial possibilities. How do you choose the most appropriate ones for your needs? Well, because it will look best if you tie it into some element already present in your decorating scheme, start by taking cues from the rest of the furnishings.

Wooden Poles

A wooden pole might match or complement the finish of the woodwork or wood furniture in the room. Can't find a match from all of the varieties of wooden poles available? Then, stain an inexpensive pine pole in a finish to match what you need. If your room features painted furniture or colorful furnishings, paint the pole as well as any rings

A stick serves as a pole for plain curtain panels with tie tabs, above. The combination fits perfectly with the other rustic elements of this bedroom, from a picket-fence headboard to a worn bench at the foot of the bed.

Drapery poles are supported by the brackets fastened to the window frame or wall. The brackets that are provided with the poles generally coordinate and blend in with the pole finish. Brackets can be simple but also decorative. If you opt for a spectacular, attention-grabbing bracket, consider choosing less showy finials for the ends of the pole.

The pole with decorative finials, above left, supports draperies hung from rings. **A twig,** above, serves as a bracket for a stick pole. **A family of birds** and their nest, left, sits above a panel hung with red clothespins.

that will slide along it. Be aware that you can buy or replicate on a wooden pole practically any finish that you might find on wood, including stained, painted, gilded, pickled, marbled, and verdigris finishes.

Metal Poles

If you're leaning toward a metal pole, zero in on the metallic elements in the room to help you determine which type will best suit the room. You may not think many are present, but a careful look around will demonstrate otherwise. Study the picture frames, lamps, switch plates, and fireplace screens and tools. And don't forget to look at decorative panels, collectibles, ceiling fan hardware, heat registers, and radiators. If the room has a predominance of gold or brass accents, as is often the case in traditional rooms, choose a brass pole. Perhaps it's a contemporary setting, or one that features silver, pewter, or wrought iron, where a brushed chrome pole would look best. Rustic rooms accented with folk art and Americana are natural homes to wrought-iron poles, but this metal can also be an eye-catching contrast in many contemporary rooms.

Finials

Unless you want to repeat an element or motif in your room, simply choose a finial you like. You may fancy a finial's shape or texture so much that you'll want to repeat it as a motif elsewhere in the room. The variety of finials seems endless, but common designs include fleur-de-lis, shepherd's crook, ball, spear, urn, acorn, flame, twig, acanthus leaf, and scroll motifs. Typical finial materials are wood and metal, and they usually match the material of the pole with which they are paired. Sometimes, though, the finial provides a contrast to the pole. Ceramic and glass finials, for example, stand out like jewels against their typically metal rods. Elaborate finials that would be too

Delicate branches painted gold, above right, hold lightweight panels. **Twisted wood and colorful rings and finials,** opposite, are perfect for these curtains. **A sunny holdback,** right, peeks out from behind yards of fabric.

Because they're designed to stand out, decorative poles and their finials require more room for installation than conventional drapery rods. Finials add inches to the ends of a window treatment, so make sure you have enough wall room to display your hardware to its full advantage. And because decorative rods are often heavy, be certain your window frames and walls can support the additional weight.

Installing Rods and Poles

The way to install a rod or pole depends on the type it is, the brackets that will hold it, the weight of the window treatment, and the surface to which it is being fastened. Given below are some general guidelines, but for specific installation procedures, refer to the instructions that accompany the rod or pole.

- Use a stepladder to reach high places.
- Use the proper tools.
- Take accurate measurements.

- Work with a helper.
- If attaching a bracket to wood, first drill small pilot holes to avoid splitting the wood.
- Consider using wall anchors, particularly for the heavier window treatments.
- Use a level as needed to help you position the brackets for the pole or rod.
- Take care not to drill or hammer into any pipes or electrical wiring.

A plain holdback, left, is used as a swag holder. A simple curtain ring and a fleur-de-lis hook, above, combine to hold back a panel banded with a bold plaid. The metal rod with glass finials, opposite, reiterates the chrome and silver accents gracing the table below it.

heavy in metal are frequently made of a plastic resin or another lightweight composite and finished to resemble metal or another substance.

RINGS, CLIPS, PINS

Most curtain and drapery panels are attached to a pole through the use of rings or clips. With them, you can open or close the treatment at will. Certain lightweight panels are secured in place with decorative drapery pins. These treatments, however, are stationary.

Rings and Clips

Drapery rings slide along a pole and are the means for connecting the drapery or curtain panels to the pole. For best results, the ring finish, of which there are many, should coordinate with that of the pole. The method for attaching the panel will depend on the type of ring. One kind has a small clip for grabbing the fabric directly, and another has a small ring for receiving a hook already in

place at the top of the panel. Others open like rings used for hanging shower curtains, fastening around a rod and into buttonholes or grommets in the top of the panel.

Pins

Pins are like scaled-down, knob-styled holdbacks, and they're used to fasten smaller amounts of lightweight fabric permanently in place. Available in a range of decorative styles and materials, pins can be used to instantly create such top treatments as swags and scalloped valances. You can also use them to hold up a lightweight curtain.

HOLDBACKS

Holdbacks can be hooks, pegs, or knobs in various materials and motifs, many of which are meant to coordinate with or match a decorative finial. With most treatments, each piece of a pair of holdbacks is mounted to a side of the window so it's ready to support a pulled-back curtain or drapery panel. A holdback may also serve

Concealed Rods

Some window fashions just look better when hung from concealed rods. Here's an overview of some types of rods.

Bay window rod. This single- or double-rod variety eliminates the need for each window of a bay window unit to have separate hardware.

Ceiling-mounted rod. This rod attaches to the ceiling or the underside of a window frame. It can be useful for hanging window treatments in tight spaces like corners and dormers.

Combination rod. A pair of two or a set of three stationary rods that share the same brackets, these rods accommodate multiple layers of rod-pocket treatments.

Continental rod. This is a wide stationary rod for a window treatment having a rod-pocket opening of equal width to the rod. It can also be used to make a decorative rod sleeve.

Corner rod. Available in single- or double-rod versions, a corner rod eliminates the problem of lining up separate hardware that meets exactly on windows set into a corner.

Double-track rod. The same concept as a traverse rod (below), a double-track rod has two tracks for layering window treatments. A triple-track version is also available.

Swivel rod. Also known as a French door rod, this hinged rod is ideal for treatments that can swing out of the way on occasion.

Tension rod. This adjustable rod has rubber tips and a built-in tensioning device so that it can sit within the window frame.

Traverse or concealed-track rod. This rod provides a track onto which drapery is hooked and, through the use of a cord system, can be drawn open and closed. It can also be bent to fit a particular contour.

Wire or cable rod. Great for curved or angled areas, this consists of a metal cable threaded through brackets on the wall.

as a "hook" for a working tieback. The level at which to install holdbacks depends on the look you want. Do you prefer the panels pulled back high, at the middle of the window, or somewhere in between? When installing holdbacks, be sure they'll be hidden behind the panels when they're not in use. Holdbacks can also serve as swag or scarf holders.

Ornate swag holders and tasseled ties, above, contain this billowy arrangement. **These swag holders,** opposite, differ in style but not in color or purpose.

SWAG &
SCARF HOLDERS

Decorative swag and scarf holders add more pizzazz to an already beautiful top treatment. Swag and scarf holders can be plain holdbacks or complex brackets that come complete with instructions for incorporating rosettes into the swag or scarf as you hang the material across the window. And although a decorative pole is not typically thought of as a swag holder, swags can be beautifully draped over one or wrapped across it. (See "Window Scarves," page 59, for more information.)

Another type of swag and scarf holder is a decorative bracket, sometimes referred to as a corbel or sconce when used for this purpose. Often made to imitate beautifully ornate architectural elements, brackets can be very formal in nature, but in an otherwise plain room, they become the defining detail. Usually made from plaster or resin composites, these brackets are installed at the top of the window or door to either the wall or casing and are structured with an opening through which a swag or a drapery rod can be threaded. The brackets are available prefinished in various looks or as plain white ones that can be tailored to fit your specific decorating scheme.

Decorative hardware can be traditional or inventive.

Use your imagination to create your own artful hardware. Make a pole from a tree branch that's not too heavy but sturdy enough to support your fabric. Paint a new finish on a store-bought bracket to match your décor. Lightly sand the bracket and wipe it with a tack cloth before applying the new paint and stain.

Details make the difference.
That's why it's so exciting to
find such an array of styles in
poles, finials, holdbacks, and
tiebacks in today's market.
Use these items to underscore
your decorating theme,
whether it is rustic country,
Old World elegant, clean-lined
contemporary, or refined
American traditional.

finishing touches

Flourishes such as trims, tassels, or tiebacks **finish** a window treatment and give it a **professional** look.

There are many types of finishing touches that can be added to a window treatment to give it a rich, professional look that captures the eye and sets it apart from the rest. Even just one carefully chosen embellishment can transform an otherwise perfect window treatment into a unique, hard-to-overlook feature in a room.

If you are purchasing custom-made window treatments, incorporating these details is simply a matter of taking the time to select trimmings to match the fabrics and hardware. If you're buying ready-made treatments or constucting them yourself, you can embellish them with store-bought or handmade trims and accents. It's not that difficult to do. Besides time and a bit of patience, you'll need the basic ability to stitch, fuse, or glue the trims in place. That's it. Craft and some fabric stores will have the supplies. Your challenge will be in trying to narrow down your choices from the outstanding selection of trimming materials and colors. The best advice: keep it simple and choose a design that is in keeping with the style of the fabric and the room. Reserve ornate details for traditional fabrics and formal interiors.

You may find it useful to sketch ideas before deciding finally what size and shape works the best with your design. In many instances, the window treatment itself will lead you in the right direction. For example, you may want to accentuate the pretty shape of a scalloped edge with trim. To focus attention on the meeting point of a set of swags, add a rosette.

Design Tip

If conventional trims and braids don't excite you, look for untraditional or unusual elements for decorating your window treatments. Attach single beads, small shells, or crystal drops at regular intervals along the edge. Either glue them in place or, if they have holes, sew them on. A series of stars, leaves, or some other appropriate shape made of stiffened fabric and then glued or stitched on is another idea. Consider old or new buttons, jewelry, or metal chains. If your embroidery skills are good, use them to embellish the window treatment.

Tassels

Tassels, whether alone or as part of a tieback, are often the crowning touch of a window treatment. Available in a wide range of sizes, styles, colors, and materials, they basically consist of long strands of thread (often silk) that are tied and folded in half and then wrapped tightly just beyond the fold. Below the tie is the skirt of the tassel. Often a casing encloses the top of the tassel. Fancy tassels might have brass, chrome, pewter, or gilt tops; ceramic and carved wood tassel tops are also available. The strands of thread in the top and skirt can be partitioned and tied or decorated in a tremendous variety of ways to increase the beauty and complexity of the tassel. Tassel varieties include the key tassel, a large tassel with rows of smaller tassels all around it, and the frog tassel, which features a pair of tassels falling below a series of decorative loops and is further embellished with a rosette.

TRIMS

A trim of any kind—braid, fringe, ruffles, piping— can further enhance the personality of almost any window dressing, whether it is a curtain or drapery panel, a top treatment, or a shade. It can match or contrast with the color, pattern, or texture of the fabric; it can be placed along its edge or at an appropriate area on the face of the treatment. All of these factors combine to build the look you want for the treatment. For example, ornate braiding or opulent fringe on a heavy drapery panel can back up a period treatment beautifully. A gathered, matching-fabric ruffle along an edge will soften the look of even a

Tasseled fringe, above, restates the colors of the drapery panel. **Tassels,** opposite, are just one of the types of embellishments used for this unusual valance.

Design Tip

You don't have to limit yourself to tiebacks made from matching or contrasting fabric. Achieve creative custom looks by making tiebacks from unexpected items. Some materials to consider are old cotton bandannas or silk scarves, strings of beads, lengths of leather, or old belts and chains.

lightweight curtain, giving it a fussy, feminine feeling, while a pleated ruffle will bring a formal, traditional note to a curtain. Rickrack trim applied to the face of a treatment or inserted into the seam along its edge is playful and casual—perfect for a child's room, a playroom, a modern kitchen, or a rustic den. Simple bands of contrasting fabric trim following the edge can reiterate and perhaps reinforce the edge so that it can stand up to more tugging over the years.

Choosing Trims

When selecting a trim, choose one having the same care requirements as the fabric in the panel and of a weight that will not overwhelm it. Bring a sample of the fabric with you to match it with the trim. If your plan is to embellish ready-made curtains, buy an extra panel and make your trim from it. If you're making your own panels and fabric trim, buy adequate yardage.

Applying Trims

Some trims—flat braids, ribbons, appliqués—can be applied to the face of the window treatment; others—piping, cord with a selvage—are meant to be inserted into a seam. To fasten trim to the face of a window treatment, use a fusible web product, hot glue and a glue gun, or a special fabric adhesive. The better method,

Beads, opposite, add sparkle and glamour to a plain curtain. **Piping and a pleated ruffle,** above left, form a distinctive edge finish. **Three fabric ties,** above, with pinked edges are simple in form but elegant in look.

Types of Trimmings

Despite the enormous variety of trimmings available, certain types, as listed below, appear over and over in window treatments. Perhaps you'll find them to be just what you need.

Ruffles. A strip of gathered fabric; a double ruffle features two layers of frill. For a pleated ruffle, the fabric is pressed into neat folds. Both edges of a ruffle can be finished; if the ruffle is for insertion into a seam, only one edge is finished.

Picot Braid. A flat braid patterned with small loops or scallops along one or both edges.

Cord. Yarns or strings twisted together to form a rope. Thick cord is typically used for tiebacks.

Flanged Cord. Cord having a selvage for inserting the trim into a seam.

Fan-Edge Braid. A flat trim with a straight upper edge and a lower edge with an open fanlike pattern formed by looped cords.

Piping. Folded bias-fabric strip, often covering cord, that is inserted into a seam so only a portion of the folded edge is visible. Also known as welting.

Fringe. A trim having a braided upper part and a lower portion of lengths of cord that are patterned in various ways. Many types of fringe are available; the name usually describes the effect formed by the fringe. Here are a few examples.

- **Brush fringe** has a row of thin cords, cut to form a straight, brushlike edge.
- **Bullion fringe** is a thick fringe made of uncut twisted cord.
- **Campaign fringe** is made up of one or more rows of bell-shaped tassels.
- **Tasseled fringe** is a type of brush fringe, but the strands are grouped and tied together at regular intervals along the length of the trim.
- **Minitasseled fringe** is made of a row of brush fringe overlaid with small tassels.
- **Onion fringe** is a tasseled fringe with a tie at the bottom of each tassel to produce bulblike shapes.
- **Looped fringe** positions the cords in a definite open-loop pattern.

however, is to sew it in place using hand or machine stitches before adding a lining fabric, if there is one. You have more control, the staying power is usually stronger, and if need be, it will be easier to remove the trim later.

ROSETTES

A rosette is a decorative window accessory typically placed between swags or where a swag meets a jabot or a valance reaches a panel. One might also be used as part of a tieback treatment. Made from fabric, usually to match that of the curtain or drapery, a rosette is ruffled or folded to form a roselike pouf that's then attached to the window treatment. The rosette can take a wide variety of forms. Common rosette styles are the *choux* (cabbage), fabric rose, and Maltese cross. If you're going the custom route, a fabricator might present you with design sketches of other shapes. If you want rosettes to complement a ready-made treatment or curtains you are making, purchase an extra panel or additional yardage from which you can fashion your own. Because edges require finishing and many fabrics are not reversible, creating rosettes usually requires sewing skills. Many home sewing project books can give you step-by-step instructions for fashioning all kinds of rosettes, and there are easy patterns you can buy. Or try the Maltese cross, referring to "Making a Simple Rosette," on page 86.

Scarf Rosettes

Typically, the rosette is a separate item that is attached once the rest of the window treatment is in place. Today, however, the rosettes that we see most often are those formed using special hardware that is designed specifically to accommodate scarf treatments. Unlike traditional rosettes, these are formed from the scarf fabric itself while it is being draped across the window. When considering this type of scarf, remember to add extra fabric, about 10

Custom-made fabric roses, left, coordinate in fabric and are defining features for this swag treatment.

to 15 inches per rosette, to the total yardage necessary for the window scarf. Specific instructions for creating the rosettes are included with the specialty hardware.

Without the special hardware as an aid, you can create rosettes for a scarf by knotting the material at the appropriate points. Start out with a small knot, and then loosely knot the material over it until it looks generous. Once you've created the rosette, you can primp it and tack it in place. Before buying fabric, knot it to determine how much will be required for each rosette. Lightweight gauzy fabrics that have no right or wrong side work best with this treatment.

TIEBACKS

Besides being decorative, a tieback holds in place curtains or draperies that have been pulled back, usually to the side of a window. In this way they are similar to holdbacks. (See "Holdbacks," page 70.) There are three main categories of tieback—fabric, braided, and tasseled—and within each category is a wide range of styles, one more attractive than the next.

Tiebacks are typically attached to hooks installed discreetly on the window frame. Rings, loops, or ties on the ends of the tieback are the usual means for fastening it in place. A tasseled tieback, however, because it is a loop of cord, simply latches on to the hooks. For a more decorative approach, a tieback can be hooked over stylish knobs or peg holdbacks.

Positioning Tiebacks

The beauty of this style of window treatment is in the lines and curves formed in the draping of the curtain panels. Most treatments use two tiebacks, one for each half of the window covering. The preferred location for

Buillon fringe and tasseled tieback, opposite, restate the colors in the fabric. **Tassels,** one plain, above right, and another ornate, right, dress these panels beautifully.

Making a Simple Rosette

One of the simplest rosettes to make is a Maltese cross. For each cross, you will need 24 inches of a wide, sturdy reversible ribbon (such as wired ribbon) that complements the window fabric; a 4-inch-square swatch of window fabric; a 3-inch-square piece of cardboard; a few cotton balls; a stapler and staples; a hot glue gun and glue; and scissors. Work on a hard, flat surface.

- Cut the ribbon in half, and arrange the two strips in a cross pattern. Staple the strips together at the center. Then fold all four ends of the ribbon to the center, and staple them in place. For a fuller Maltese cross, add more 12-inch lengths of the same ribbon or other colored ribbons to the cross, and position them diagonally to form an X. Fold these ribbon ends to the center, and then staple them in place.
- Cut a 2-inch-diameter circle from the cardboard, and staple it once to the center of the cross. Glue two or three cotton balls onto the cardboard circle, and let them dry. Then, with the right side of the window fabric swatch up, cover the cotton-padded cardboard with the fabric, tucking and gluing the edges of the fabric onto the reverse side of the cardboard. Let the rosette dry, and then pin or sew it in place.

hooking tiebacks is slightly above or below the center of the window. A low placement makes a window appear taller than it really is; a high tieback creates a tight, short curve of fabric. Another effective treatment is to use multiple tiebacks drawn to the same side of the window but hooked at different levels. Before installing any hooks, decide where you want the tiebacks. Experiment by pulling back the curtain or drapery at various spots until you find what looks best for the window and room.

Fabric Tiebacks

Most fabric tiebacks are flat strips, stiffened with buckram or fusible interfacing and lined. Plain or fancy in shape, fabric tiebacks can match exactly, coordinate with, or provide a contrast to the curtain panels they hold. Fabric tiebacks are suitable candidates for all the same trimmings as window panels. You can sew piping into the edges, add fabric bands, or border panels with ruffles. For a formal effect, attach tassels or fringe.

For a very simple bow tieback, wrap a long length of wide ribbon around the panel, and tie its ends into a bow, positioning it at a strategic point of the panel. Then, "hook" the ribbon onto the holdback or hook.

Simple in design yet stylishly attractive is a ruched tieback. It consists of an inner core of buckram or thick cord covered by a sleeve of fabric that is twice the length of the cord. The extra fabric creates a soft, gathered effect along the length of the tieback.

Braided Tiebacks

A braided tieback comprises three or more strands of decorative cord or fabric-covered cord that are plaited together. A braid made from silky cord of jewel tones interspersed with gold strands will look rich, upscale, and formal, while cords covered in a calico print will be a perfect choice for a casual country-style window treatment. For a contemporary room setting, consider braiding lengths of wire or leather cord; for a romantic theme, use strings of beads.

Tasseled Tiebacks

Usually formal in nature, tasseled tiebacks are lengths of cord featuring either a single tassel in the center of the tieback or a pair of tassels, one on each each end. They are available in a range of colors and weights of cord. The tassels can be simple or ornate, and match or contrast with the cord. (See "Tassels," page 78.)

Striped fabric and grommets, opposite, combine to form an effective trim for this curtain. The choice of grommet used in holding back the panel will alter the drape.

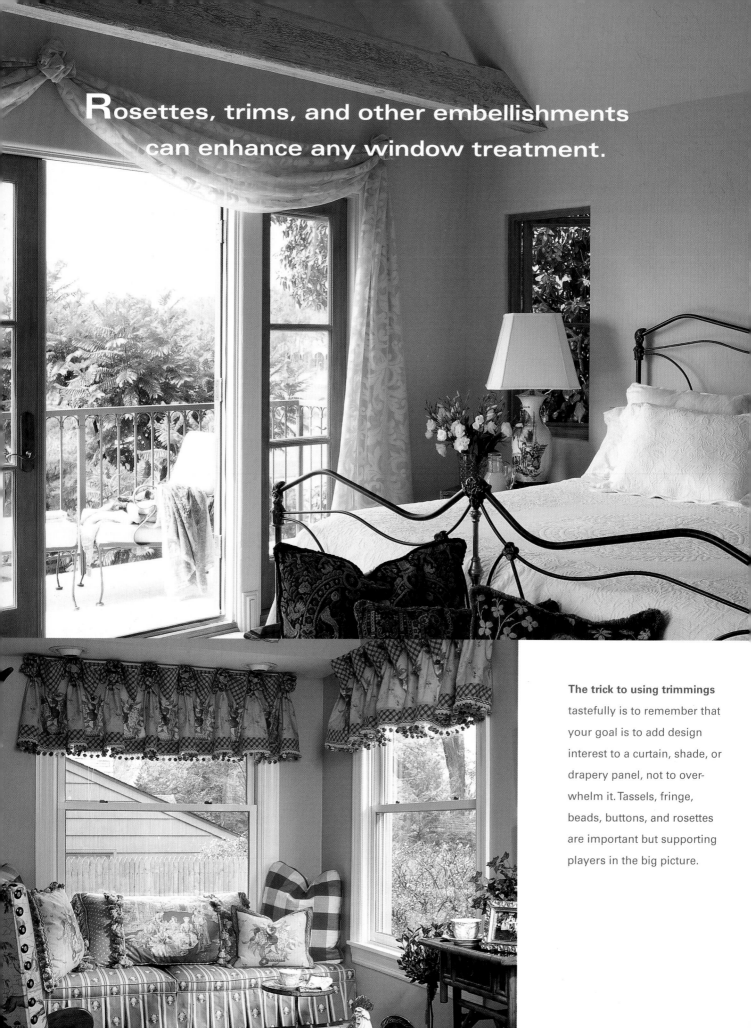

Rosettes, trims, and other embellishments can enhance any window treatment.

The trick to using trimmings tastefully is to remember that your goal is to add design interest to a curtain, shade, or drapery panel, not to overwhelm it. Tassels, fringe, beads, buttons, and rosettes are important but supporting players in the big picture.

7

challenges
& solutions

Whether it's due to **size,** shape,
or **location,** some windows can
be a challenge to **treat.**

Certain windows typically pose problems. These include bay, bow, casement, and dormer windows; too large, small, tall, or short windows; and specialty or unusually shaped windows, such as cathedral, round, elliptical, arched, or triangular units. Occasionally even ordinary windows, particularly when they are at corners or are different in size and shape from the other windows in the room, can be a challenge to dress properly. Glazed doors, because of their movement, have other needs. Sometimes the answer is the installation of special hardware. (See "Concealed Rods," page 72, for more information.) Other times you can rely on the creative use of fabric or decorative elements to solve the problem.

A window treatment that is well designed will remove any awkwardness of the window and shift your focus from the problem to the decorative quality of the treatment itself. Alternatively, if the shape of the window is more important, then the window treatment could be an accent rather than the focus. The first step in successfully dressing a difficult window is to consider all types of coverings—curtains, shades, valances, swags and jabots, and so on—imagining them on the window and visualizing what they accomplish. Try combining the types, by adding a valance over a shade or a set of side panels, for example. Make a pencil sketch of the window as a base and then, using tissue-paper overlays, sketch various arrangements, adding embellishments as needed to complete a look. As you shop for the elements and trims, attach samples to your drawing, making note of the prices and sources.

BAY & BOW WINDOWS

Bay and bow windows are multiple-window units that project out from the exterior wall of a house to form a recessed area inside the house. The primary difference between the two is that the recess of the bay window is angled, whereas the bow window's is curved.

There are several options for dressing a bay window. A casual treatment might consist of dressing each window in the unit with a valance on top and then a shade, blind, or set of café curtains on the bottom. Another solution is

Each bay window setting, opposite and below, is dressed differently to suit style, light, and privacy concerns.

Design Tip

Occasionally too little room exists between the window frame (if there is one) and the ceiling. In this situation you might be able to use ceiling-mounted hardware. Alternatively, a cornice across the top and a rod mounted inside the cornice will give you the dual benefit of visually lowering the top of the window and concealing the hardware.

to hang curtain panels from a single bay window rod installed directly above all the windows. The bay window rod is essential because individual rods above the windows would be crowded for space, and the treatment will not flow. Using a double bay window rod, a traditional formal treament could consist of a pair of curtain panels for each window opening hanging from the inside rod and two drapery panels—one at each end of the unit—from the outer rod. Another choice is to hang drapery panels and a top treatment on a straight rod, fastened outside and across the top of the recess of the window unit.

A bow window generally requires the use of a curved rod installed directly above all the windows of the unit. It's a custom item well worth the investment because from it you can hang anything from a full drapery treatment to a simple top treatment. Professionally bent traverse rods, also called concealed track rods, are even more versatile. Another option for a bow window is a wire or cable rod that will take on the shape of the curve. They are best suited for lighter-weight treatments.

Both bay windows, left and opposite, have a treatment inside the alcove; **the bay,** opposite, has another outside.

Visual Tricks

Some windows can be difficult to treat just because they're not the right size or proportion. Several of these dilemmas can be solved with fool-the-eye tricks. Other times it will be a matter of using a treatment that does not conform to the precise measurements of the window.

To make a wide window appear narrower

- Use a fabric the same color as the wall.
- Hang side panels within the frame of the window.
- Use a treatment whose lines will break up the horizontal line of the window.

To make a narrow window appear wider
- Extend the treatment beyond each end of the window.
- Use tieback curtains, which tend to add width visually.

To make a tall window appear shorter
- Use a longer, fuller top treatment.
- Cap it with a valance having points or lines that will pull the eye downward.

To make a small window appear larger
- Install a treatment that extends just beyond the dimensions of the window. If the treatment is movable, as is a shade or blind, don't go too far beyond the actual size of the window, because the difference will be very apparent when the treatment is open.

CASEMENT & DORMER WINDOWS

A casement window, which opens out, presents no special problems in terms of window covering. Keep in mind, however, that you will want easy access to the crank handle that operates the unit. A good choice for any casement window is to hang panels from swivel rods, which allow you to swing the panels out of the way when you need to open the window.

A dormer window, because it's recessed in an alcove and has a wall on each side of it, leaves little room for treatments such as draperies that stack when they're open. One solution is to hang panels from swivel rods. Another is to install your hardware outside the alcove and choose a window treatment—a valance and two side panels, for example—to frame the whole area.

CORNER WINDOWS

Windows that converge at the corner of a room look best when treated as a unit. When dressing them, use any elements you would use for a pair of windows adjacent to each other on a flat wall. If you want to "join" the two and make the corner the focus, hang a drapery panel on each outer edge and a set to fill the space in the corner between the windows. Corner rods available in double- or single-rod versions eliminate the awkwardness of installing separate rods on each window, and they ensure that your treatment will fill in the corner of the wall without leaving a gap. Try mirror-imaging two halves of a treatment. For example, cover each window with a tieback curtain or drapery panel, and pull each panel to the outside edge of the window. Another successful look is achieved by dressing the windows with swags and jabots, setting a pair of jabots at the corner.

A **ceiling-mounted rod,** opposite, and **a cornice,** above right, are features of these corner-window treatments. **A simple shade,** right, adorns a small window.

SPECIALTY WINDOWS

Various shaped windows, such as arched, round, half-round, elliptical, and angular, sometimes placed above one or more large windows, are favorites with new-house builders. Aesthetically, it is usually best to leave as much as possible of these beautiful windows unadorned because their pleasing shapes and muntins are meant to be on display. Perhaps a valance or a creatively draped scarf is all that's needed. On the practical side, however, this does not allow for the control of light, especially sunlight and its glare and heat, nor does it provide privacy. This could be particularly problematic if the window is large, as is a cathedral window or the arch-topped Palladian window.

If you must cover an "architectural" window, there are options. You can buy custom cellular shades for many

Specialty windows, left, below, and opposite, are best when unadorned or dressed simply with treatments that can be moved aside to fully reveal the window's features.

Design Tip

Some windows are set so close to corners that no area exists for certain treatments such as draperies that stack when they are open. One possible solution is to use lightweight panels, which are less bulky when they are stacked. Otherwise, choose coverings that are confined to the limits of the window—blinds, shades, café curtains, valances, or even swags and jabots.

configurations. Shutters are another made-to-order option, although you can sometimes purchase ones that will fit standard-size windows. Kits allow you to create a rod-pocket curtain for a variety of window shapes, but any one of these curtain treatments is fairly stationary once it is in place. For an angled window, consider shirred curtains on ordinary adjustable rods affixed to the top and bottom of the window or on tension rods set within the window frame. An arched rod is another option to investigate for a window with a curved top. Available in a large variety of sizes, an arched rod allows you to treat an arched window as you would a square or rectangular unit. You can install the rod as you would an ordinary one, mounting it inside or outside the window opening. Once the treatment is up, however, it is stationary.

To enjoy the architectural beauty of a large specialty window such as a cathedral or arch-top Palladian-style window but still have some light control, consider a covering for the lower portion only. Use a treatment, such as draperies on rings and a decorative rod, that can be drawn open or closed at will.

GLAZED DOORS

The most important consideration for any treatment on a glazed door is that all the elements will clear the opening and not interfere with the operation of the doors. The quintessential treatment for sliding glass patio doors and French doors that open out is draperies on a decorative or traverse rod. Long panels puddled at the floor, however, aren't suitable because they may catch onto the bottom of a sliding door.

If the doors open into the room, you also have to pay attention to the top of the treatment so that it won't interfere with the door swing. When the wall space above the door is adequate, you could top it with a valance or a scarf wrapped around a pole. Or consider sheer sash curtains that attach directly to the doors. Another alternative is to hang panels from swivel, or French door, rods.

One long decorative rod, below, set high above French doors, supports draperies on rings. **Woven-wood shades,** opposite, provide a unified look for dissimilar windows.

Possible Solutions for Challenging Windows

Some windows are more difficult than others to dress. Frequently the solution is in the form of specialty hardware. Other times it involves a unique placement of ordinary hardware and the treatment. Listed below are some suggested ways for treating these windows.

Type	Solutions
Bay Window	• Use a specially designed bay window rod. • Place a treatment outside the alcove. • Treat windows singly, perhaps each with a shade and a simple top treatment.
Bow Window	• Use a curved rod, a professionally bent traverse rod, or a wire or cable rod.
Casement Window	• Try swivel rods (sometimes called French door rods) to swing the treatment out of the way when necessary.
Corner Window	• Use a specially designed corner window rod. • Use a wire or cable rod. • Try mirror-imaging two halves of the treatment.
Dormer Window	• Try swivel rods to swing the treatment out of the way when necessary. • Hang the treatment outside the alcove.
Glazed Door	• Use panels that cover only the windows of the door. • Install a traverse rod above the opening and make sure the treatment and its stack back clear door openings. • Try swivel rods to swing the treatment out of the way when necessary.
Specialty Windows	• Use bent-rod kits designed for round, elliptical, octagonal, arched, or eyebrow windows. • Use custom cellular shades or shutters.

Blend your ingenuity and design skills when dressing a challenging window.

Thanks to specialty blinds, shades, and shutters, a window of any size or shape can be fitted for privacy and light control if they are concerns. More often than not, pairing a hard treatment with a soft one is the solution because it can be versatile. But no matter what type of challenge a window presents, it also offers the opportunity to pull together a look that makes the window the focal point in the room.

8

minimal
looks

Sometimes **less** is more when it comes to choosing the **right** window **treatment** for its surroundings.

Rooms with a minimal or uncluttered look can be striking in their simplicity, emphasizing space and architecture rather than decorative objects, prints, or patterns. To a decorating minimalist, one who prefers clean lines and fewer personal effects, layers of fabric, buttons, bows, and showy hardware go against the grain. If you prefer an unfussy interior with open and airy windows or you live in a contemporary clean-lined house, you need a minimal window treatment—one that reinforces the lines and perhaps textures already present in the architecture and interior surfaces.

Dressing a window to coordinate with a minimal design scheme does not mean limiting the solution to a plain blind or a simple top treatment, although these are options, especially for informal rooms. Some minimal environments are complex and formal, however, and call for window treatments to echo that. Also typical of this style are large windows or a wall of glass, where the treatment must be an unobtrusive frame for a good-looking window, an accompaniment to the elements inside the room, and a controlling device for light and air. In some cases, a sheer or translucent covering is all you need. Other times the best treatment can be none at all, particularly if there's a great view outside and privacy isn't a concern.

In this chapter you'll see how simple or streamlined window fashions provide the perfect solution to numerous interior design situations. In addition, you'll find inspiration for creating unique looks with unexpected objects.

CONVENTIONAL TREATMENTS

Line definition plays an essential role in a minimal environment. Instead of focusing on busy, colorful upholstery and window treatments, your eye follows the geometry of the surfaces and furniture in the room. The architectural features are more likely to stand out in an uncluttered room, too. For this reason, hard elements that can add lines or restate ones that are already in play are natural choices. Contrary to what you may think, soft elements such as fabric are not taboo in a minimal setting. The type of fabric you choose and how you use it, however, can make or break the design scheme.

Hard Elements

Used alone, window treatments such as blinds, shades, shutters, and cornices work well in a minimal setting.

Louvered blinds or fitted shutters offer optimal light regulation and privacy in a minimal environment, and the louvers of either are easily adjustable. You can choose vertical or horizontal blinds according to what suits the room. Natural shade types such as matchstick, bamboo, and other woven woods, reeds, grasses, and synthetic look-alikes offer interesting light play and texture. If you're also using curtains or draperies, you might choose a translucent fabric so that the line play of the shade, blind, or shutter is not lost behind the fabric.

As the day progresses, the muntins of a window with multiple panes provide the geometric structure for a play of shadows that travel on the floor and the wall opposite the window. An angled skylight can also be the force

Roman shades, opposite and above, work well in minimal settings. When they're open, the window, room, and view share the glory. When closed they provide privacy.

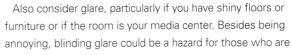
behind another light-and-shadow show. Curvy lines present in a minimal room can be echoed and emphasized by the look of light shining through a window that is framed by a cornice or lambrequin, the edges of which are shaped to restate these curves in the room or to add a sensuous element to a rectilinear space.

Soft Elements

Minimalist designs can also rely on the power of textures to create interest. When choosing a fabric for a window treatment, look for one with a surface that invites you to touch it. Raised damask or brocade tone-on-tone fabrics with patterns that tie in with something else in the room are examples, as well as some linens. Heavy or coarse fabrics and materials with distinctive patterning such as tweeds or twills are also possibilities. Avoid floral prints, busy patterns, frilly laces, and any fabrics that will defeat your contemporary or spare design goals—reserve such fabrics for a traditional or country room.

Other appealing choices for this style of interior are sheer see-through fabrics. Sheers are versatile. They can be tailored or relaxed, patterned or plain. Long curtain or drapery panels made from a sheer fabric can add a simple sculptural shape to an otherwise boxy window. Sheer materials are also great for the way they soften the light streaming through them, sometimes also providing

a shadowy display of the structure and lines of the window or door right behind them.

In terms of color, curtains and draperies are often best when kept neutral or subtle in color, sometimes with a tone-on-tone look. Pattern and lively prints, unless they are geometric, should be avoided because they can be distracting. Remember, your goal is to make the window treatment unobtrusive and let the space itself, the window's architecture, or the view take the spotlight.

Hardware

When choosing decorative hardware for a spare design, look for choices that are simple, elegant, and harmonious with furnishings or accents already present. Avoid ornate styles, especially elaborate finials. Brushed-metal finishes look most appropriate, but wood painted to blend in with a window's frame and trim works well, too. If you are using holdbacks, keep to simple styles that will not detract from the rest of the overall design. Resist any temptation to add accents that will defeat your intention to make either the window itself or the window beyond it the focus of attention.

The sheer curtains, opposite, are a simple, soft decoration for these second-story bedroom windows and the panorama of nature beyond them. In such a secluded spot, privacy concerns are minimal at best.

OTHER "MINIMAL" TREATMENTS

When you can't produce a minimal treatment using conventional components, try using elements that are not thought of as typical window dressings. Some suggestions are given here. They are not presented as how-to projects but simply to inspire you to create unusual but minimal window treatments of your own. Instructions and supplies for making some of them are available in craft stores.

Grilles and Grids

Metalwork can be stunning and, with light behind it, casts lovely images onto the floor or an opposite wall. You can sometimes find vintage grillwork at antique stores or where architectural salvage is sold. Shoji screens, made of wood framing and textured papers, imbue a room with understated elegance and pattern. Sections of old weathered picket fencing are another possibility for adding texture. New fencing and latticework, finished to suit the room, can also work.

Stained and Leaded Glass

Scour antique shops and art-glass stores for stained- or leaded-glass panels that you can suspend in front of or set into your windows. Depending on the weight of the glass and the way you install it, this may be a choice more suitable for stationary windows. You might also want a professional to install the panel.

Glasswork, Beads, and Shells

Where strong light is not a problem, shelves of colored glasswork or strings of pretty beads provide some coverage while creating interesting color and light reflections inside the room. Strings of shells can do the same. Choose your elements with a sense of proportion to the window, reserving fine, delicate objects for small openings and big ones for larger windows. As always, trying to achieve proper scale and proportion is often a trial-and-error process, so be patient and experiment until you get the desired effect.

Plants

When properly chosen for their care and light needs, plants can flourish as a window decoration that adds fresh natural color to an interior. Try various shapes and heights of plants. Look for ones with interesting fronds or leaves that can create patterns in front of a window or provide some privacy. To accommodate hanging plants, suspend a shelf from the ceiling or from wall brackets, varying the height of the shelf according to the area the plants will cover. Or display the plants in hanging baskets. Install decorative hooks, using anchors for adequate support. Plants, especially large ones, can get very heavy after watering.

A stained- and leaded-glass window, right, is the focal point here. An antique metalwork piece, opposite above, makes a stunning window decoration. A red-and-white valance, opposite right, hides a closed miniblind.

Design Tip

You can easily stencil a work of art onto a windowpane, perhaps only as a border around the edge. Choose or create a design that gives you as little or as much privacy and light control as you need. Use a ready-made stencil or a piece of openwork fabric such as lace, or mask a design onto the glass using tape and a razor knife. Then apply glass paint or frosted glass spray, referring to the instructions and guidelines that come with the product.

Protecting Your Privacy

Often with the sparse unadorned features of a minimal window treatment, your privacy becomes a concern, particularly at night and for bedrooms and baths. Here are some things to do to make sure you are not inviting the curiosity of passersby.

• Stand outside the house and look at your window to see whether more covering is needed. You might want to do this during the day and again at night with the lights on in the room before you make a decision to leave a window bare or partially treated.

• Install an opaque, movable treatment to cover the lower part of a street-level window, the entire surface of a below-street-level window, or all or part of a high-rise-apartment window, depending on what you need to ensure your privacy.

• Consider putting frosted or one-way glass into all of the windows or just into those areas needed to provide privacy.

• Investigate automatic controls for opening and closing the window treatment at the appropriate times.

A minimal treatment can be the best look for certain settings.

Window treatments that are
barely there or starkly simple can
be appealing alternatives to
layered or "constructed" window
fashions, especially if the
architecture of the window itself
is interesting. Beautifully shaped
specialty windows or stained-
and leaded-glass panels work
well in a minimal setting.
Lightweight sheer or lace
curtains will allow filtered light
inside without completely
sacrificing privacy. Adjustable
shades that roll up and are
almost out of sight when not
needed are another option for a
spare design. Or try a simple
valance or sheer scarf swag for
an understated but pretty look.

resource guide

Associations

American Architectural Manufacturers Association *is an organization of window, door, and skylight manufacturers. The Web site offers a listing of window products and a section on national window safety.*
1540 East Dundee Rd., Suite 310
Palatine, IL 60067
Phone: 708-202-1350
www.aamanet.org

American Sewing Guild *is a nonprofit organization for people who sew. Members receive discounts for sewing-related materials.*
9660 Hillcroft, Suite 516
Houston, TX 77096
Phone: 713-729-3000
Fax: 713-721-9230
www.asg.org

Home Sewing Association *directs the sewer to projects, press releases, discussions, and sewing-related links.*
1350 Broadway, Suite 1601
New York, NY 10018
Phone: 212-714-1633
www.sewing.org

Window Covering Association of America *is a nonprofit trade organization for the window-covering industry. Its Web site offers tips, patterns, a Q & A message board, and a dealer directory.*

WCAA National Office
2339 Meadow Park Ct.
St. Louis, MO 63043
Phone: 888-298-9222
www.wcaa.org

Window & Door Manufacturers Association *promotes high-performance standards for windows, skylights, and doors.*
1400 E. Touhy Ave., Suite 470
Des Plaines, IL 60018
Phone: 800-223-2301
Fax: 847-299-1286
www.wdma.com

Manufacturers & Retailers

Soft Treatments

Country Curtains *specializes in curtains and accessories, with ideas and tips on the Web site.*
Country Curtains at The Red Lion Inn
Stockbridge, MA 01262
Phone: 800-456-0321
www.countrycurtains.com

Croscill Home Fashions *manufactures curtains and decorative hardware.*
261 Fifth Ave., 25th Floor
New York, NY 10016
Phone: 919-683-8011
www.croscill.com

Romanzia *creates custom-made fabric shades and valances. The customer provides the fabric.*
655 County Rd. A
P.O. Box 72
Chetek, WI 54728
Phone: 715-924-2960
Fax: 715-924-4244
www.romanzia.com

Smith & Noble *makes custom soft and hard window treatments.*
1801 California Ave.
Corona, CA 92881
Phone: 800-560-0027
www.smithandnoble.com

Spiegel *catalog's home accents collection offers everything related to window treatments: curtains, blinds, valances, and accessories, such as tiebacks, sconces, and decorative rods and finials.*
Spiegel Customer Satisfaction
P.O. Box 6105
Rapid City, SD 57709
Phone: 800-474-5555
www.spiegel.com

Waverly *manufactures fabrics and ready-made curtains. The Web site includes tips on how to decorate effectively and a product finder.*
Phone: 800-423-5881
www.waverly.com

Hard Treatments

BTX Window Automation, Inc. *manufactures motorized systems for window coverings.*
10880 Alder Circle
Dallas, TX 75238
Phone: 800-422-8839
Fax: 214-343-2252
www.btxinc.com

Hunter Douglas, Inc., *manufactures shades and blinds. The Web site will direct you to designers, dealers, and installers.*
2 Park Way
Upper Saddle River, NJ 07458
Phone: 800-937-7895
www.hunterdouglas.com

Levolor Home Fashions *manufactures blinds and shades, including cordless types.*
4110 Premier Dr.
High Point, NC 27265
Phone: 336-812-8181
Fax: 336-881-5862
www.levolor.com

The Pillow Parlor *sells ready-made decorative cornices and canopies for windows.*
56 North Federal Hwy. (U.S. 1)
Dania, FL 33004
Phone: 800-954-1515
www.pillowparlor.com

resource guide

Smith & Noble *(See Curtains & Soft Treatments.)*

Southwestern Blind Company *sells a wide variety of ready-made blinds.*
P.O. Box 10013
Austin, TX 78766
Phone: 888-792-5463
Fax: 512-331-9000
www.swblind.com

Spiegel *(See Soft Treatments.)*

Hardware

Atlas Homewares *sells decorative hardware. Ideas for unique tiebacks are found on the Web site.*
326 Mira Loma Ave.
Glendale, CA 91204
Phone: 800-799-6755
www.atlashomewares.com

Graber Window Fashions *manufactures curtain hardware. All questions can be answer by e-mail.*
www.graber.ws/index.html

Kirsch Window Fashions *manufactures blinds, rods, shades, holdbacks, and other window accessories in a variety of styles. The Web site has a glossary of various window treatment terms.*
524 W. Stephenson St.
Freeport, IL 61032
Phone: 800-817-6344
www.kirsch.com

Ona Drapery Company *manufactures rods, brackets, tiebacks, finials, and other accessories.*
5320 Arapahoe Ave.
Boulder, CO 80303
Phone: 800-231-4025
Fax: 303-786-7159
www.onadrapery.com

Fabric

Ainsworth Noah & Associates *sells fabric.*
351 Peachtree Hills Ave., Suite 518
Atlanta, GA 30305
Phone: 404-231-8787
www.ainsworth-noah.com

Benartex Incorporated *supplies cotton fabric designs from a variety of original collections.*
1460 Broadway, 8th Floor
New York, NY 10036
Phone: 212-840-3250
Fax: 212-921-8204
www.benartex.com

Calico Corners *sells a selection of fabrics and offers custom services in its stores nationwide.*
203 Gale Ln.
Kennett Square, PA 19348
Phone: 800-213-6366
www.calicocorners.com

F. Schumacher & Co. *manufactures fabric and coordinated wallcovering.*

939 Third Ave.
New York, NY 10022
Phone: 212-415-3900
www.fschumacher.com

Joann Fabrics and Crafts *sells fabrics, notions,
patterns, and craft products in its stores nationwide.*
5555 Darrow Rd.
Hudson, OH 44236
Phone: 888-739-4120
www.joann.com

J.R. Burrows & Co. *supplies hand-printed art
fabrics and lace, with reproductions from many
design periods.*
6 Church St.
Boston, MA 02116
Phone: 617-451-1982
www.burrows.com

Motif Designs *manufactures fabric and
coordinated wallcovering.*
20 Jones St.
New Rochelle, NY 10802
Phone: 800-431-2424

Old World Weavers *carries fabrics made of wool,
cotton, silk, and more.*
D&D Building
979 Third Ave.
New York, NY 10022
Phone: 212-752-9000
Fax: 212-758-4342
www.old-world-weavers.com

Plaid Enterprises, Inc., *manufactures craft and
home decorating products including fabric and glass
paints, stamps, stencils, paints, and stitchery
supplies.*
P.O. Box 2835
Norcross, GA 30092
Phone: 800-842-4197
www.plaidonline.com

Rashmishree *makes tassels, ribbons, and trims.*
P.O. Box 723
Pine Brook, NJ 07058
Phone: 973-808-1566
www.rashmishree.com

Sahco Hesslein *is an international textile
manufacturer that creates original fabrics.*
3720 34th St.
Long Island City, NY 11101
Phone: 718-392-5000
www.sahco-hesslein.com

Scalamandré *manufactures and imports fabrics
and trimmings.*
300 Trade Zone Dr.
Ronkonkoma, NY 11779
Phone: 800-932-4361
www.scalamandre.com

Waverly *(See Soft Treatments.)*

glossary

Apron: Molding installed at the bottom of a window, below the inside sill, or stool.

Austrian Shade: An opulent style of shade that hangs in cascading scallops from top to bottom. Often made of a sheer or lacy fabric, it is raised by a cord.

Balloon Shade: A fabric shade that falls in full blousy folds at the bottom; it is raised by a cord.

Bay Window: A multiple-window unit projecting out from the exterior wall of a house, forming an angled recess inside the house.

Bow Window: Similar to a bay window, but the recess is curved.

Box Pleats: Two folds turned toward each other, creating a flat-fronted pleat.

Brackets: Hardware to support a curtain or drapery rod or pole or, as with a scarf swag, a decorative holder for the treatment.

Brocade: A weighty, typically formal fabric in silk, cotton, wool, or a combination of these fibers. Woven on a Jacquard loom, it is distinguished by a raised, typically floral, design.

Buckram: A coarse, stiff fabric used as an interlining to give body and shape to curtain and drapery headings, cornices, and tiebacks.

Café Curtains: A window treatment that covers only the bottom portion of a window. Panels are most often hung at the halfway point of the window.

Calico: Lightweight, inexpensive cotton or cotton-blend fabric in brightly colored prints.

Casement Window: A hinged vertical window that opens out; often operated with a crank mechanism.

Cathedral Window: A triangular or trapezoidal window paired with and placed above a large fixed window. The top portion of a cathedral window is often left uncovered.

Chintz: A cotton fabric, typically having a floral or other overall print, coated with a resin to give it sheen.

Cloud Shade: A balloon shade having a gathered or pleated heading.

Combination Rods: Two or three rods sharing one set of brackets. They facilitate the layering of various treatments, such as draperies over sheers.

Cornice: A projecting decorative boxlike unit installed above a window, designed to hide a curtain rod.

Damask: A jacquard fabric of cotton, silk, wool, or a combination, woven with a raised design. Widely used for draperies and top treatments.

Dormer Window: A window set into the front face of a dormer. A dormer window brings light into the space provided by the dormer.

Double-Hung Window: The most common type, consisting of two sashes, one atop the other, which are moved up and down to open and close the window.

Draping: A technique of folding, looping, and securing fabric in graceful curves and lines.

Draw Draperies: Draperies that hang from a traverse rod and can be drawn to open or close over the window by means of a pulley.

Face Fabric: The main outer fabric of a window treatment, as opposed to its lining.

Festoon Shades: A class of adjustable or stationary shades that are made of gathered fabric. Styles include balloon, cloud, and Austrian.

Finials: The decorative ends of a drapery rod or pole.

French Doors: Two adjoining doors with hinges at

opposite ends and typically with 12 divided panes of glass in each door.

Fringe: A decorative trim attached to curtain panels, draperies, top treatments, and other window coverings as an embellishment.

Gingham: A light- to medium-weight, plain-weave fabric yarn dyed and woven to create checks or plaids.

Goblet Pleat Heading: A heading with tube-shaped pleats that are pinched together at their bases.

Heading: The horizontal area at the top of a curtain or a drapery. Its style determines how a curtain or drapery looks and hangs.

Holdback: Hardware (made of metal, wood, or glass) that is attached to the wall near the edge of a window and is used to hold in place a pulled-back curtain or drapery panel. It can also be used as a swag holder.

Interlining: Lightweight opaque fabric placed between the face and lining fabrics of a drapery to add body or to block light.

Jabot: The vertical tail that complements a swag in a swag-and-jabot treatment.

Jacquard: The name of the inventor and of the loom that revolutionized weaving by using punched cards to produce jacquard fabrics, which have intricate, raised designs. Brocade and damask are jacquard fabrics.

Lambrequin: A painted board or stiffened fabric that surrounds the top and sides of a window or a door.

Lining: A fabric added to the window treatment for body and a visually unified exterior appearance. It also helps to control light, air, and dust that filter through the window.

Moiré: A silk or acetate fabric having a finish that resembles watermarking.

Mounting Board: A wooden board installed either inside or outside the window frame to which some types of window treatments are attached.

Muntin: Wood trim that sets off smaller panes of glass in a window.

Muslin: A plain-weave cotton fabric ranging in weight from coarse to fine.

Piping: An edging trim made of folded bias-cut fabric, which is sewn into a seam. It often encases cord. Also known as welting.

Pleated Shades: Shades made of permanently folded paper or fabric.

Pole: Metal or wooden hardware that supports curtain or drapery fabric; also called a rod.

Repeat: The duplication of a design motif or pattern at consistent or random intervals in a fabric.

Return: The distance from the front face of a curtain or drapery rod to the wall or surface to which the brackets for the rod are attached.

Rod: See Pole.

Rod-Pocket Curtains (or Draperies): Panels that hang from a rod threaded through a stitched pocket across the top of the panel. The most common window treatment.

Roller Shade: A shade made of vinyl or fabric attached to a spring-loaded roller.

Roman Shade: A fabric shade that forms layers of straight, flat horizontal folds when open. It is lifted by pulling a cord threaded through rings attached to fabric tape on the back of the shade.

Ruching: Extremely tight gathers used as a decorative top finish to a panel.

glossary

Stack Back: The space along the sides of a window or door taken up by a curtain or drapery panel when it's pulled open.

Swag: The center drape or scallop of fabric in a swag-and-jabot treatment; it can have a deep or shallow drop.

Tab-Top Curtains (or Draperies): Panels that hang from a rod via looped fabric tabs.

Taffeta: A shiny silk or acetate fabric that maintains its shape. It is used for formal curtains and draperies.

Tail: A common term for jabot, the vertical lengths of fabric that complement a swag.

Tieback: A cord or fabric strip used to hold open curtains or draperies.

Toile de Jouy: An eighteenth-century print of pastoral scenes on cotton or linen, printed in one color, usually on a white background. It was first produced in Jouy, France.

Traverse Rod: A rod that opens and closes the window treatment by pulling a cord.

Valance: A short length of fabric that hangs along the top of a window, with or without a curtain, drapery, or other treatment underneath.

Venetian Blind: A blind made of metal or wood slats, attached to cloth tape, and worked by a cord on a pulley.

Welting: See Piping.

index

A

Angled skylight, 107
Arched rod, 42, 100
Austrian shade, 26
Austrian valance, 40

B

Balloon shade, 26
Balloon valance, 40
Bay window rod, 72, 94, 101
Bay windows, 93–94
   rods for, 72, 94, 101
   window treatments for, 93–94, 101
Beads, in minimal treatments, 110
Bell-pleat valance, 40
Blinds, 25, 29–33
   custom versus stock, 31
   horizontal, 107
   inside mount for, 32, 34
   louvered, 107
   in minimal treatments, 107
   outside mount for, 32, 34
   pairing with curtains, 31
   Venetian, 29, 31
   vertical, 32–33, 107
Bow windows, 93–94
   rods for, 72, 94, 101
   window treatments for, 93–94, 101
Box cornices, 42–45, 47
Box-pleat valance, 40
Braided tiebacks, 86
Brocade, 21
   in minimal treatments, 109
Brush fringe, 82
Bullion fringe, 82
Butterfly pleat, 17
Butterfly-pleat valances, 40

C

Cable rod, 72, 94, 101
Café curtains, 14
   for bay windows, 93
Café shutters, 34
Cambric, 21
Campaign fringe, 82
Canvas, 21
Cascade jabot, 59
Casement windows, 97
   rods for, 72, 97, 101
   window treatments for, 97, 101

Ceiling-mounted rod, 72, 93, 97
Cellular shades, 29
Challenges and solutions, 90–103
Chintz, 21
Choux rosette, 83
Clips, 70
Cloud shade, 27
Cloud valance, 40
Color, in minimal settings, 109
Combination rod, 72
Concealed rods, 72
Concealed-track rod, 72, 94
Continental rod, 72
Corbels, 73
Cord, 82
Corner rod, 72, 97, 101
Corner windows, 97
   rods for, 72, 97
   window treatments for, 97, 101
Cornices, 38, 42–47, 93
   box, 42, 45, 47
   making simple, 46
   in minimal settings, 107, 109
   shaped, 45
Crown swag, 55
Curtains
   café, 14
   distinguishing from draperies, 10
   fabric types for, 21
   headings for, 10, 14–20
   pairing blinds with, 31
   panels, 13–14
   tiered, 14
Curved rod, 94, 101

D

Damask, 21
   in minimal treatments, 109
Decorative hardware, 64–75
   brackets, 46, 67
   clips, 70
   finials, 68, 70
   holdbacks, 64, 70, 72
   installing, 69
   in minimal designs, 109
   pins, 70
   poles, 66–70
   rings, 70
   rods, 72
   swag and scarf holders, 73
Decorative poles, 66–70
Dormer windows, 97
   rods for, 72, 97, 101

   window treatments for, 97, 101
Doors, French, 100
Doors, glazed, 100
   rods for, 72, 100, 101
   window treatments for, 100, 101
Doors, sliding, 100
Double swags, 55
Double-track rod, 72
Draperies
   distinguishing from curtains, 10
   fabric types for, 21
   headings for, 10, 14–20
   panels, 13–14

F

Fabric rosette, 83
Fabrics, 21
   sheer, in minimal settings, 109
   sun damage and, 109
   for tiebacks, 86
   for window scarves, 59
   for window treatments, 21
Fan-edge braid, 82
Fan pleat, 17
Faux-wood blinds, 31
Festoon shade, 26
Finials, 67–70
Finishing touches, 76–89
Flanged cord, 82
Flat headings, 18–19
Fluted jabot, 59
French door rod, 72, 100, 101
French doors, 100
Fringe, 82
   brush, 82
   bullion, 82
   campaign, 82
   looped, 82
   minitasseled, 82
   onion, 82
   tasseled, 82
Frog tassel, 78
Frosted glass, 111

G

Gathered headings, 17
Gathered valances, 42
Gingham, 21
Glare, 109
Glasswork, 110
   leaded, 110
   stained, 110

index

Glazed doors, 100
   rods for, 72, 100, 101
   window treatments for, 100, 101
Goblet pleat, 17
Grids, 110
Grilles, 110

H

Hardware, decorative, 64–75, 109
Headings, 10, 14–20
   flat, 18–20
   gathered, 17
   pierced, 20
   plain, 20
   pleated, 17
   pocket, 17
   rod-pocket, 17
   tab-top, 18
   tie-top, 18
Holdbacks, 64, 70, 72
Honeycomb shades, 29
Horizontal blinds, 107

I

Inside mount, 34
   measuring windows for, 32
Interlining, drapery, 13

J

Jabots, 50–63
   cascade, 59
   fluted, 59
   pipe, 59
   plaids and stripes for, 56

K

Key tassel, 78

L

Lace, 21
Lambrequins, 45
   in minimal settings, 109
Leaded glass, 110
Light, amount of, 109
Line definition, role of, in minimal
   setttings, 107
Linen, 21
Lining, drapery, 13
Looped fringe, 82
Louvered blinds, 107
Louvered shutters, 34

M

Maltese cross rosette, 83, 86
Metal poles, 68
Metalwork, 110
Minimal looks, 104–113
   beads in, 110
   color in, 109
   decorative hardware for, 109
   fabrics for, 109
   glasswork in, 110
   grilles and grids in, 110
   hard elements in, 107–109
   hardware for, 109
   leaded glass in, 110
   line definition in, 107
   plants in, 110
   protecting privacy in, 111
   shells in, 110
   stained glass in, 110
   textures in, 109
Minitasseled fringe, 82
Mirror imaging, 97
Moiré, 21
Molding, for a box cornice, 45
Muntins, 107
Muslin, 21

O

One-way glass, 111
Onion fringe, 82
Organdy, 21
Outside mount, 34
   measuring windows for, 32

P

Palladian-style window, 100
Panels, 13–14
   interlining for, 13
   length, 13–14, 20
   below-sill, 14
   floor length, 14, 17
   puddled, 14
   sill, 13, 22
   lining for, 13
Panel shutters, 34
Pelmets, 38
Pencil pleat, 17
Picot braid, 82
Pierced headings, 20
Pinch pleat, 17
Pins, 70
Pipe jabot, 59

Piping, 82
Plaids, for swags and jabots, 56
Plain headings, 20
Plantation shutters, 34
Plants, in minimal treatments, 110
Pleated headings, 17
Pleated shades, 26–29
Pleated valances, 40
Pleats
   butterfly, 17
   fan, 17
   goblet, 17
   pencil, 17
   pinch, 17, 48
Pocket headings, 17
Poles
   decorative, 66–70
   installing, 69
   metal, 68
   wooden, 66, 68
Privacy, protecting your, 111
Puff valance, 40

R

Rings, 70
Rod-pocket headings, 17
Rods
   arched, 42, 100
   bay window, 72, 94, 101
   cable, 72, 94, 101
   ceiling-mounted, 72, 93, 97
   combination, 72
   concealed-track, 72
   continental, 72
   corner, 72, 101
   curved, 94, 101
   double-track, 72
   French door, 72, 100, 101
   inside mount for, 32
   installing, 69
   outside mount for, 32
   swivel, 72, 100, 101
   tension, 72
   traverse, 72, 101
   wire, 72, 94, 101
Roller shades, 27, 33
Roman shades, 27, 107
Rosettes, 83–85, 88
   making simple, 86
   Maltese cross, 83, 86
   scarf, 83, 85
Ruffles, 82

index

S

Satin, 21
Scarf holders, 73
Scarf rosettes, 83, 85
Scarf swags, 59–61
Sconces, 73
Shades, 25, 27–29
    Austrian, 27
    balloon, 27
    cellular, 29
    cloud, 27
    festoon, 27
    honeycomb, 29
    inside mount for, 32, 34
    natural, 107
    outside mount for, 32, 34
    pleated, 26–29
    roller, 26, 33
    Roman, 27, 107
    room-darkening, 29
    woven-wood, 29
Shaped cornices, 45
Sheer fabrics, in minimal
    treatments, 109
Shells, in minimal treatments, 110
Shoji screens, 110
Shutters, 25, 33–34, 100
    café, 34
    louvered, 34
    in minimal settings, 107
    panel, 34
    plantation, 34
    wooden, 34
Silk, 21
    sun damage and, 109
Skylight, angled, 107
Sliding doors, 100
Specialty windows, 98–100, 101
Stained glass, 110
Stencils, 111
Sun damage, 109
Swag holders, 73
Swags, 50–63
    crown, 55
    double, 55
    holders for, 73
    number of, 52, 55
    plaids and stripes for, 56
    scarf, 59, 60–61
    single, 55
    styles of, 52–59
    three or more, 59

    triple, 51, 59
    width of, 52
Swivel rod, 72, 97, 101

T

Tabbed valances, 42
Tab-top headings, 18
Taffeta, 21
Tasseled fringe, 82
Tasseled tiebacks, 85, 86
Tassels, 78, 85
Tension rod, 72
Tiebacks, 81, 85–86
    braided, 86
    fabric, 86
    positioning, 85–86
    tasseled, 85, 86
Tiered curtains, 14
Tie-top headings, 18
Toga valances, 42
Toile de Jouy, 21
Traverse rod, 72, 94, 101
Trims, 78–83
    applying, 78, 81–83
    choosing, 78, 81
    types of, 78-81, 82
Triple-pleat valance, 40
Triple swag, 51, 59
Tweeds, in minimal treatments, 109
Twills, in minimal treatments, 109

V

Valances, 38, 40–42
    Austrian, 40
    balloon, 40
    bell-pleat, 40
    box-pleat, 40
    butterfly-pleat, 40
    distinctive, 41
    gathered, 42
    pleated, 40
    pleated-and-gathered, 40
    puff, 40
    tabbed, 42
    toga, 42
    triple-pleat, 40
Velvet, 21
Venetian blinds, 29, 31
Vertical blinds, 32–33, 107
Visual tricks, 94

W

Welting, 82
Windows
    bay, 72, 93–94, 101
    box, 72, 93–94, 101
    casement, 72, 97, 101
    challenging to treat, 90–103
    corner, 98, 101
    dissimilar windows, 100
    dormer, 72, 97, 101
    measuring, 32, 34
    Palladian-style, 98, 100
    specialty, 98–100, 101
Window scarves, 52, 59–63
    wrapping, 60–61
Window treatments. See also
    Windows.
        for bay windows, 93–94, 101
        for bow windows, 93–94, 101
        for casement windows, 97, 101
        for corner windows, 97, 101
        for dissimilar windows, 100
        for dormer windows, 97, 101
        fabrics for, 21
        for glazed doors, 100, 101
        in minimal settings, 104–113
        protecting your privacy with,
            111
        for specialty windows, 98–100,
            101
        visual tricks with, 94
Wire rod, 72, 94, 101
Wooden poles, 66, 68, 109–110
Wooden shutters, 34
Woven-wood shades, 29
Wrapped scarves, 60–61

credits

page 1: Robert Harding Picture Library page 2: Giammarino and Dworkin page 5: Robert Harding Picture Library page 6: Mark Lohman page 7: *top to bottom* Jessie Walker; Brad Simmons; Robert Harding Picture Library; Jessie Walker page 8: Tria Giovan page 11: Giammarino and Dworkin page 12: Robert Harding Picture Library page 14: *top to bottom* Mark Samu; Tria Giovan page 15: Robert Harding Picture Library page 16: Nancy Hill page 18: *top to bottom* Mark Lohman; Mark Samu page 19: Brad Simmons page 20: *all* Robert Harding Picture Library page 21: Scalamandré page 22: *top* Jessie Walker; *bottom left* Robert Harding Picture Library; *bottom right* Brad Simmons page 23: *top to bottom* Mark Lohman; Tim Street-Porter/Beate Works page 24: Mark Lohman page 26: *all* Robert Harding Picture Library page 27–31: *all* Mark Lohman page 32: Tim Street-Porter/Beate Works page 33: Mark Lohman page 34: *left* Jessie Walker; *right* Mark Lohman page 35: Mark Lohman page 36: *top* Mark Lohman; *bottom*

Giammarino and Dworkin page 37: Phillip Ennis page 39: Mark Lohman page 40: *top to bottom* Jessie Walker; Mark Samu page 41: Mark Samu page 42: Jessie Walker page 43: Phillip Ennis page 44: Mark Lohman page 45: *top to bottom* Jessie Walker; Mark Lohman page 46: Jessie Walker page 47: Mark Samu page 48: *top and bottom left* Mark Lohman; *bottom right* Mark Samu page 49: *top left* Jessie Walker; *top right* Nancy Hill; *bottom* Mark Samu page 50: Mark Samu page 52: *all* Mark Lohman page 53: Jessie Walker page 54: Mark Lohman page 55: *all* Mark Samu page 56: Mark Lohman page 57: Mark Lohman page 58: Mark Lohman page 59: Mark Samu page 60: *all* Jessie Walker page 61: Mark Lohman page 63: *top left* Nancy Hill; *top right and bottom* Mark Lohman page 65: Mark Samu page 66: Giammarino and Dworkin page 67: *top and middle* Mark Samu; *bottom* Jessie Walker page 68: *top* Nancy Hill; *bottom* Mark Lohman page 69: Jessie Walker page 70: *left* Mark Lohman; *right* Jessie

Walker page 71: Mark Samu page 72: Tim Street-Porter/Beate Works page 73: Mark Lohman page 74: *left* Jessie Walker; *right* Mark Samu page 75: *top and bottom left* Mark Samu; *top right* Mark Lohman; *bottom right* Robert Harding Picture Library page 76: Time Street-Porter/Beate Works page 78: Jessie Walker page 79: Tim Street-Porter/Beate Works page 80: Giammarino and Dworkin page 81: *top* Mark Lohman; *bottom* Jessie Walker page 82: *top right* Scalamandré; *center* Mark Samu page 84: Mark Lohman page 85: Giammarino and Dworkin page 87: Tria Giovan page 88: *top* Grey Crawford/Beate Works; *bottom* Jessie Walker page 89: *top left* Jessie Walker; *top right* Mark Lohman; *bottom* Brad Simmons page 90: Mark Lohman page 92: Mark Lohman page 93: Mark Samu page 94–95: *all* Mark Lohman page 96: Mark Samu page 97: *top to bottom* Mark Samu; Mark Lohman page 98: *top* Tria Giovan; *bottom* Mark Samu page 99: Mark Lohman page 100: Phillip Ennis page 101: Mark Lohman page 102–103: *all* Mark

Lohman page 104: Jessie Walker page 106: Mark Samu page 107: Mark Lohman page 108: Mark Samu page 109: Giammarino and Dworkin page 110: Jessie Walker page 111: *top* Mark Lohman; *bottom* Brad Simmons page 112: *top* Mark Samu; *bottom* Mark Lohman page 113: *top* Robert Harding Picture Library; *bottom* Tria Giovan page 120: Mark Samu page 122: Mark Lohman page 125: Tim Street-Porter/Beate Works

Have a home improvement, decorating, or gardening project? Look for these and other fine Creative Homeowner books at your local home center or bookstore.

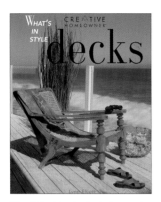

The latest in deck design and deck products. More than 200 color photos and illustrations.
128 pp.; 8½"×10⅞"
BOOK #: 277183

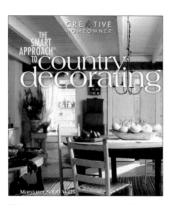

Fill your home with the spirit of country: fabrics, finishes, and furniture. More than 200 photos.
176 pp.; 9"×10"
BOOK #: 279685

Transform a dated kitchen into the spectacular heart of the home. Over 150 color photos.
176 pp.; 9"×10"
BOOK #: 279935

How to work with space, color, pattern, and texture. Over 300 photos.
256 pp.; 9"×10"
BOOK #: 279667

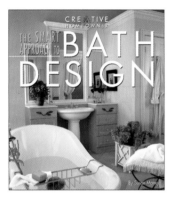

All you need to know about designing a bathroom. Over 150 color photos.
176 pp.; 9"×10"
BOOK #: 287225

Get the practical information you need to choose window treatments. Over 100 illustrations & 125 photos. 176 pp.; 9"×10"
BOOK #: 279431

Turn an ordinary room into a masterpiece with decorative faux finishes. Over 40 techniques & 300 photos. 272 pp.; 9"×10"
BOOK #: 279550

Interior designer Lyn Peterson's easy-to-live-with decorating ideas. Over 350 photos.
304 pp.; 9"×10"
BOOK #: 279382

Impressive guide to garden design and plant selection. More than 600 color photos.
320 pp.; 9"×10"
BOOK #: 274615

Lavishly illustrated with portraits of over 100 flowering plants; more than 500 photos.
208 pp.; 9"×10"
BOOK #: 274032

Everything you need to know about setting ceramic tile. Over 450 photos and illustrations.
160 pp.; 8½"×10⅞"
Book #: 277524

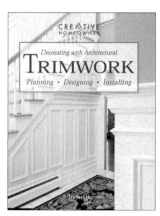

How to create a richly textured home. More than 450 color photos and illustrations.
208 pp.; 8½"×10⅞"
BOOK #: 277495